SCENES FROM THE HISTORY

OF THE PORTUGUESE IN GUYANA

FAR; FAR AWAY THY CHILDREN LEAVE THE LANDE
'Longe, longe teus filhos a terra deixão'

(O Imparcial, No. 238. Sexta Feira, 28 de Marco 1845)

Three Generations of Portuguese
Leonora Coelho-Menezes and her son, José Coelho. Menezes
from Madiera: José C-Menezes' small daughter, Henriqueta Menezes

Scenes from the History of the Portuguese in Guyana

by

Mary Noel Menezes, RSM

(150th ANNIVERSARY PUBLICATION)

Published by Sister M N Menezes, RSM
William Goodenough House
Mecklenburgh Square
London WC1N 2AN

ISBN: 0 9511531 0 2

Printed by Victoria Printing Works (Kingston) Ltd
Kingston upon Thames, Surrey, England

ACKNOWLEDGEMENTS

So many thanks are due to so many people who gave generously of their time to make this book a reality. Warm appreciation to Sister Celine Marie, Sandra Seenan and Doreen De Caires who spent many laborious hours copying the relevant documents in the National Archives, Guyana; to John Simon De Freitas and Sandra Granger who helped with the translation; to Grace Daniels who typed much of the material; to Joyce Callaghan who helped with the proofing; to Audrey and M T Lowe for the photography and printing; to Vibrant Cambridge for his interest and support, and, above all, to my many Portuguese friends for their encouragement and inspiration.

PREFACE

The aim of this book, as previously mentioned in my lecture on the Portuguese given at Bishop's High School on 29 April, 1985, is two fold:

First, to educate the Portuguese presently living in Guyana or those who have lived in Guyana, regarding their cultural heritage, their historic legacy. According to Cicero, the famed 2nd century BC Roman orator, philosopher and statesman: 'Not to know what happened before we were born is to remain perpetually a child, for what is the worth of a human life unless it is woven into the life of our ancestors by the records of History.'

Secondly, to educate our fellow Guyanese and other ethnic groups and so sharpen the awareness of the valuable political, economic, social, cultural and religious contributions of each group without which there would be no viable history of Guyana.

I maintain that these aims should not be relegated only to the history of our Portuguese people but should also be the goal of serious historical investigation of the other ethnic groups, the African, the East Indian and the Chinese who entered Guyana over the past centuries and formed our plural society. In my writings on the Amerindians I feel I have acquitted such a debt to those people who rightly hold pride of place in Guyana.

This book is dedicated to the more than 30,000 of our Portuguese ancestors and many others who during the nineteenth century braved the rigours of Atlantic travel to settle in an unknown and far off land, to those who died in this country and those who became outstanding citizens and not only economic but cultural and religious contributors to this complex society of ours.

24th September 1985.   M Noel Menezes. RSM

CONTENTS

SELECTED CHRONOLOGY OF
HIGHLIGHTS IN HISTORY
OF PORTUGUESE IN GUYANA – 1835-1985

1835,	3 May	–	Arrival of first group of 40 Madeirenses
1842	–	–	Stoppage of Portuguese emigrants
1843	–	–	First import of goods by Portuguese on the 'Zargo' (wines esculents and fancy articles)
1845	–	–	First Portuguese priest in Colony – Senhor Joaquim Antonio Correa de Natividade
1846	–	–	Resumption of large-scale immigration
1847,	May-1848		Portuguese shops pillaged in New Amsterdam
1850s	–	–	Rising commercial success of Portuguese
1856,	18 Feb		'Angel Gabriel' riots vs Portuguese
1861,	25 Dec		Sacred Heart RC Church opened
1865	–	–	Portuguese Female School established – forerunner of Sacred Heart School
1870	–	–	St John the Baptist Church, Plaisance, opened
1875	–	–	Portuguese Benevolent Society established
1876	–	–	'Primeiro de Dezembro' Band established
1882	–	–	D I H opened (Mr João Fernandes)
1884	–	–	G Bettencourt and Co Ltd
1886	–	–	Portuguese Mutual Pawnbrokery Co of B G Ltd
–	–	–	J P Santos and Co Ltd
1889	–	–	Portuguese owned 54 out of 55 spirit shops in Georgetown
1889,	March	–	'Cent Bread' Riots
1893	–	–	Portuguese open flour factory in Pomeroon
		–	Portuguese celebrate Papal Jubilee (Leo XIII)
1895	–	–	Lusitania Cricket Club formed
1896	–	–	Lusitania Ice Co Ltd formed
			Alec Russel and Co Ltd (oldest commission house in WI)
1898	–	–	D'Aguiar Bros Ltd established
		–	Portuguese celebrate 400th Anniversary of Vasco da Gama's voyage to India
		–	Establishment of Vasco da Gama Cycling Club
		–	Establishment of Estudiantina String Band

1899	–	– First Portuguese Mayor of Georgetown – Manoel L Da Costa
1900	–	– Ferreira and Gomes, Ltd
1902	–	– Peoples Pawnbrokery Co of British Guiana
1905,	25 Dec	Bells at Sacred Heart Church rang out for the first time
1909	–	– D M Fernandes, Ltd (Demerara Cycle Depot)
		– M P Camacho, Ltd
		– De Caires Bros, Ltd
1912	–	– The Park Hotel (Alexander Gonsalves)
1914	–	– Correia's Wine Factory
1915	–	– Central Garage (John De Freitas)
1917	–	– British Guiana Biscuit Factory, Ltd
1921	–	– Hon Francis Dias – first Portuguese in National Politics
1921	–	– Pestano's Outfit Store
1925	–	– Charlestown Saw Mills, Ltd (S S De Freitas)
1926	–	– De Freitas Ltd (Hardware)
1928	–	– Francis De Caires and Co Ltd (now Frandec Travel Co)
1929	–	– Schuler and Gomes – Optometrists and Opticians
		– Standard Pawnbrokery (Francisco Gonsalves Lopes)
1932	–	– Percy De Caires (now Dr) first student from St Stanislaus College to win Guyana Scholarship
1938	–	– Rodrigues and Rodrigues, Ltd
1940	–	– Portuguese celebrate eighth centenary of Portuguese nation
1942	–	– De Freitas, Ltd (Sawmills)
1948	–	– Correia's Enterprises, Ltd
1950	–	– Statue of Our Lady of Fatima brought to British Guiana by Fr Patrick Moore
1953	–	– D'Andrade Trading Co Ltd
1955	–	– Banks Breweries, Ltd (P S D'Aguiar)
1958	–	– Correia's Jewellery Ltd
1960	–	– Sacred Heart Church declared National Shrine
1967	–	– Farfan and Mendes Ltd
1970s	–	– Large exodus of Portuguese from country
1985	–	– 150th Anniversary of arrival of the Portuguese in Guyana
	29 April	Lecture – 'The Winged Impulse: The Coming of the Portuguese in Guyana'
	27 July	Portuguese Pageant and 'Feast, Food and Family' Celebration at Thirst Park.

Introduction

'The Winged Impulse: The Coming of the Portuguese to Guyana'

It is substantiated by documentary evidence that the first Portuguese coming to these shores as an immigrant group from Madeira arrived on the 'Louisa Baillie' after a 78 day voyage via London, on 3rd May 1835. What were the causes, the circumstances, both in B.G. and in Madeira, which brought these people from a very small island in the Atlantic to a distant land on the northern tip of South America? One should be familiar with the historical circumstances in the British Guiana of 1830s. The planters of the colony soon to be deprived of their slave labour by the impending abolition of slavery were desperately looking around for a substitute labour force that would be cheap, continuous and reliable. Madeira, a colony of Portugal, England's oldest ally, was then passing through dark and difficult days. It was not far-fetched for the Secretary of State, who was recommending European immigrants to fill the labour gap in B.G. to direct the planters' attention to Madeira, then suffering great poverty and political unstability. The hard-pressed peasants were undoubtedly eager to seek their fortunes in a land that was being broadcast as 'El Dorado.'

Of that first group of 40, 20 were engaged as labourers to James Albuoy of La Penitence and Liliendaal, and 20 to R G Butts of Pln Thomas. Possibly these two planters were among the more enterprising ones who privately financed immigration before bounties were payable. Two days after the arrival of the Portuguese, the editorial of the *Royal Gazette* expressed the hope: 'The competency of these islanders to perform the work expected of them is a matter of great importance to ascertain, as if the experiment is successful, it is calculated that of the 120,000 inhabitants of Madeira, at least a tithe would be willing to emigrate.' Prophetic words! Between the beginning of state-aided immigration in 1841 and its end in 1882, 30,645 Portuguese from Madeira, the Azores, the Cape Verdes, and some from Brazil had been introduced.

5

Why was there such a willingness, even maybe an eagerness on the part of the Madeiran peasant to leave his island home with its excellent climate, its beautiful mountain scenery, its serene way of life in the village, and embark on a long and uncomfortable and sometimes fatal journey?

MADEIRA AND ITS PEOPLES: TROUBLED TIMES

In the early 19th century Madeira considered 'the most beautiful gem of the Portuguese realm' had suffered from the constitutional struggles rife in Portugal. Clashes between the constitutionalists supported by João VI, and the Miguelists supporters of his son Miguel, an absolutist, led to a series of military revolts in the 1820s. Not until Pedro, João's eldest son, who had resigned his Portuguese throne to his daughter, Maria, returned from Brazil to Portugal and forced Miguel to surrender was some semblance of order felt in Portugal. Even though Maria was restored to the throne in September 1834 Portugal continued to share in the ferment that stirred Europe. Miguelism, the national debt, army revolts, and continuing civil wars racked the country until the 1850s. Madeira felt the tremors of these political, economic and military earthquakes and more than just the tremors. Between 1828 and 1834 constitutionalists and Miguelists alternately occupied Madeira. No wonder many Madeirans unwilling to take part in these struggles sought quieter climes.

Yet Madeira had had its shining hour in past centuries. Its early history is based on both legend and fact. For the romantically inclined the legendary story will intrigue. Though it is discounted in favour of the less romantic but more convincing one, the legend prefaces many a history of Madeira. In 14th century England Robert Machim, a young gentleman, fell violently in love with a lady superior to him in rank and fortune, Anne d'Arfet. His love was reciprocated but the Lady's father was not amused nor in favour of the match. Together Machim and the Lady Anne eloped in a small vessel hoping to reach France, but the sailors' ignorance of navigation drove them into the open sea. After some weeks they were tossed on a little island, made a bower under an immense tree and hoped to live there happily evermore. But happiness was short-lived; the ill-anchored vessel was swept out to sea by a gale, the lady overwhelmed died of grief and Machim did not long survive her. He begged his sailor friends to bury him near to her at the foot of the tree against which they placed a large cedar cross. Fortunately, one of the ship's boats had survived as legends will go; the sailors set off but were wrecked on the Barbary coast and enslaved. Among the slaves they met a Spaniard who when later ransomed was taken to Spain by the celebrated Portuguese navigator João Gonzalves Zargo, to whom he related the story. Zargo in turn told Prince Henry the Navigator (grandson of Edward III) who told his father, João, who then sent Zargo off post haste to find the island. This he did in fact on 10 August 1419. Later, he came across the burial spot of the lovers and named the place Machimo. Here fact merges with fiction. Inspired by the pioneering spirit of Prince Henry, Portuguese navigators were pushing the limits of the known world farther and farther in order to find a sea route to the East. Indeed Zargo did discover that island and on the instructions of João began to settle it. So completely wooded it was that he called it Madeira-island of wood. Sailing westward he discovered an excellent site for the capital; it was covered with fennel (funcho) so he named it Funchal. Zargo cleared the island of immense trees by setting fire to them, thus leaving the island barren yet the ashes greatly enriched the soil. Sturdy Portuguese peasants were among the first settlers so too were the nobility for the king sent out three young noblemen to marry with Zargo's daughters from whom descended the principal families of Madeira. Wheat was the first grown on the lush volcanic soil but after the mid-fifteenth century the prosperity of the island rested on the cultivation of the sugar cane introduced by Henry from Sicily. After 1443, slaves were introduced to work on the plantations. By 1456 the first shipment of sugar was exported to England; the 1455 production figures showed an output of 51,200 lbs per year.

MADEIRA AND INTERNATIONAL TRADE

Before the last decade of the 15th century large amounts of wheat and wine were also being produced and exported. By the time Christopher Columbus, trained in that first school of navigation, the European 'brain trust', sailed to find his gateway to the East, Madeira was already integrated into the economy of Europe and Africa. T Bentley Duncan in his book on *The Atlantic Islands, Madeira,* etc. noted:

By 1500, when Madeira had reached only its seventy-fifth year of settlement the island had become the world's greatest producer of sugar, and with its complex European and African connections, was also an important centre for shipping and navigation.

It was from Madeira that Brazil received its first sugar cane plants brought in to that country long before a similar crop was grown by the Dutch in this Guiana territory. Ironically, after 1570 the decline of Madeira sugar on the world market was due to the competition from Brazilian sugar. Other problems would jeopardise the crop: soil erosion, soil exhaustion, irrigation needs, high labour costs, destruction of the crop by rodents, insects and plant diseases.

As Madeiran sugar declined in the international trade, the wine trade superseded it. Viniculture in Madeira was again due to that indefatigable, Prince Henry, who introduced the wine from Cyprus and Crete. The result was the famed Madeira wines, enjoyed internationally then and now. Madeira was shipped around the world – St Petersburg rivalling London in number of pipes imported, and of all the British West Indian islands, Jamaica led the way. Yet the wine industry also fell on dark days. In 1884 the *oidium* and the later *phylloxera* diseases crippled the vines.

In the 286 square miles of that mountainous island Madeirans were indeed both the master and slaves of their environment. A Madeiran writer, de Goveia, highlights the attitude of the peasants when catastrophe continuously hit those crops, thus: 'the peasant, descending from the seirra with his bundle of beech sticks for the beans, and occasionally stopping to rest at the turns in the path, casts his glance at the horizon and, in spite of himself, begins to feel the winged impulse to disimprison himself in search of lands where life would be less harsh.'

Thus not only from political troubles but from what another author calls the 'pervasive tyranny of the island's geography', the Madeiran sought escape and Demerara became for him a land of hope. Both the civil and ecclesiatical authorities were apprehensive over this migratory impulse and voiced strong objections, fearful of the consequences of the population drain. But one island's loss became another country's gain. The *Royal Gazette* of May 1835 stated that the first Madeirans were proving to be 'excellent workers' impressed by both the quantity and quality of their work. The agricultural capability of the Madeiran peasant could hardly have been questioned. He was born and bred in a small mountainous island where every square inch of soil was precious. Many of the peasants owned a little piece of land or worked for the landlord – the *morgado*. On this land they grew a variety of fruits, vegetables and flowers. Madeira is called a floating garden. Therefore, one questions Henry Dalton's reasons for the Portuguese moving away from the plantations because agriculture on the island of Madeira was their forte. The first arrivals did suffer from deficiency in diet, poor accommodation, and above all, overwork in a rigorous climate in order to improve their economic status overnight. Yet neither suffering nor death deterred others from coming. Thirty of the original emigrants returned to Madeira with their earnings and encouraged their families, relatives and friends to go to Demerara; Manuel hero of "O Demerarista" was one of those returned emigrés and, as the notes to the play pointed out, the Demerarista was distinguished, not only by the copper colour of the skin but by the gold objects and by the wearing of a Panama hat! The Agent General of Madeira reported that he had almost 2,000 names of unemployed all eager to set off for British Guiana. In July 1841 Governor Henry Light wrote to the Colonial Office that the influx from Madeira was considerable and more was expected. The later introductions seems to be of a better class and Light felt sanguine that they would acclimatise more easily. By the end of 1841, 4,297 Madeirans had arrived.

The 1841 arrivals were more confident as they were coming to already established families. The July 1841 group envinced a great *joie de vivre,* embracing the sailors on their arrival at the depot at Poudroyen, and tuning their guitars, singing and dancing for hours. This love of music and dancing would be a significant contribution to the Guyanese scene, as witnessed in their religious celebrations. The festas were always accompanied by the music from the machete, rajão, guitar, and drum and fife – very similar to the type of celebration witnessed in Madeira even today. Yet 1841 proved to be a bad year for the immigrants. Yellow fever was raging in British Guiana and among the children measles spread rapidly with fatal results. As A R F Webber comments: 'The Portuguese came to a strange climate, strange food and stranger diseases.'

MORTALITY AMONG THE PORTUGUESE

Concern over the mortality of the Portuguese moved Governor Light to propose to the Court of Policy that Madeiran emigration be stopped. This policy was supported by Lord Stanley who agreed that no more emigrants be sent to the colony at the public expense. This support was obviously on the grounds of Light's strong letter regarding the 'fearful mortality' as evidenced in the returns of December 1841. However, an investigation of those returns hardly bore out the verdict of 'fareful mortality' though mortality there was. For example, on 9 estates on which 697 Madeirans were located only 31 has succumbed, including 5 out of 102 children. In over 100 estates with a total population of 2,099 – 158 had died or 7.8%. Light might not have carefully examined the returns or noted the remarks of the Stipendiary Magistrate indicating that where accommodation and medical attention were poor the death rate rose. On the other hand there was a correlation between favourable health and housing conditions and improved health. Most of the deaths reported were due to yellow fever and dysentery – the latter due to a change in diet and poor sanitation. It was noted that a few died of nostalgia!

LARGE FORTUNES FROM SMALL BEGINNINGS

Despite the mortality and the resultant stoppage of emigration from Madeira more than a 1,200 trickled in between 1841 and 1846 when large-scale bounty emigration was resumed. In 1846 the largest number ever to come to British Guiana in one year arrived – 5,975. Meanwhile the Portuguese had already begun to move off the plantations and into small farming as well as into huckster and retail trade. Although, after 1841 they would control the retail trade they never monopolised the huckster trade. Figures from the Receiver General's Office in 1845 indicated that the Portuguese held only 40.5% of the 800 huckster licenses issued. Yet the huckstering trade was not a novelty to the Madeiran. A familiar figure along the streets of Funchal was the street vendor selling onions, garlic, fruits, eggs, fish, vegetables, flowers, as well as a variety of useful objects – the trade being passed on from father to son. The Madeiran peasant knew the value of money – 'wily' was the name given them by their own countrymen; some returned to Madeira with small fortunes made from huckstering; others moved into the retail trade.

In 1843 the first import of goods by the Portuguese was made by a few who chartered a small brig, the 'Zargo'. This event, to quote the prophetic words of the *Royal Gazette* was 'likely to lead to great future changes in the commercial history of the country.' The cargo of the 'Zargo' consisted of wines, 162 boxes of potatoes, 1,000 *arrobas* of onions, as well as 15 *colonos* or labourers. It was being observed then that the rapid growth of the Portuguese was due to the assistance given them through easy credit by the mercantile firms, a concession that was never extended to the Creoles. This, stated the press, accounted for their meteoric rise in business and their becoming 'the monopolists of the retail trade in the country.' Yet, the *Gazette* conceded that the attempt of the Portuguese to enter the wholesale trade and foreign commerce showed that 'they were not destitute either of sagacity, daring or ambition.'

Here again trading and business formed part of the economic heritage of the Portuguese. The Madeirans had inherited the flair for trade from their Portuguese ancestors who had been masters in the field since the 13th and 14th centuries. In the 14th century the maritime trade of Portugual was based on the exports of salt, olive oil, fish, wine, fruit, corks, and hides to England, Flanders, the Mediterranean and Morocco.

This penchant for trade went deep and was transported to Madeira, which by the 16th century, had become an important entrepôt. Imports and exports flowed and numbers of small provision (salt goods) and dry goods stores mushroomed. Hence the Madeiran, as well as bringing his rajão, his language and his faith, brought his expertise and experience in trade. Also he longed for his *bacelhau, cebolas, alhos, arroz* and *batatas,* and his wines, all of which formed the core of his imports.

'GREAT SHOPKEEPERS OF THE COUNTRY'

At this point I would like to examine the petition of one Manuel Perreira to the Court of Policy in 1847 for compensation for the losses and suffering his wife and himself experienced when attacked by a Creole mob during some minor riots. The petition illustrates two issues in the lives of the majority of Portuguese in the mid-nineteenth century:

1. The rapid economic growth of the Portuguese century and,
2. The growing jealousy and consequent animosity of the Creoles towards the Portuguese which led to violence.

Regarding 1. Pereira had amassed the savings from the joint labour of his wife and himself (wages ranged from $8-$12 per month) while they were labourers on Pln. Houston during the first six months of their arrival in the country in December 1842. He subsequently opened a shop in Leguan and in 1846 moved to Alberttown, establishing himself in business there. Stipendiary Magistrate W Carbery reporting on the success of the Portuguese on the West Coast, Essequibo, in 1845 claimed that the shops proving unprofitable and given up by the former owner, Creole or European, were rented or purchased by a Portuguese whose activity attracted custom, while 'his superior industry and economy enable him to turn to advantage a position which the more expensive and indolent habits of his predecessor rendered profitless.' Such sentiments did not endear the Portuguese to the Creoles; on the contrary, the Creoles felt that the whites were giving 'preferential treatment' to the Portuguese who were taking the 'Bread out of their mouths'.

According to the *Official Gazette* of 1852, though the Portuguese held only 238 of the 618 huckster licenses in rural Demerara and Essequibo, they held 171 shops and stores licences out of the 296 in Georgetown; in Berbice 28 out of 52. By 1870, all of the 23 largest stores in Georgetown were owned by the Portuguese, a phenomenal growth since 1842. Yet it was in the rum retail trade that the Portuguese really made their mark. Dr M Wagner in his thesis affirmed that: 'Portuguese dominance had been first achieved within the rumshop trade.' This dominance brought about the support and encouragement of the white elite, although he conceded that within the dry goods and provision fields their success was due more to their own efforts. While not underestimating the support given to the Portuguese, their expertise in the viniculture and the production of rum was transferred to Demerara. In 1842 the first retail spirit dealer was probably John Marques of Providence. Twenty-five years later the Portuguese held 97% of the licenceses in rural Demerara; 95% in Georgetown. But times and attitudes changed. Support from the ruling elite gave way to opposition. Heavy taxation and restrictive regulations elicited strong objections from the Portuguese spirit shop dealers who did not hesitate to remind the government that they were responsible for ¼ of the entire revenue of the colony.

'OIL IN WATER: AMONG US, BUT NOT OF US.'
THE EXPLOSION OF ANIMOSITY

The rum retail trade in which very few Creoles had moved was not the rub. The *Colonist,* advertising Portuguese success, noted their entry into a variety of trades: 'The Portuguese have taken the retail provision trade out of the hands of the merchants, and they are now entering largely into the boot and shoe trade.' Their shops were flourishing; theirs was a lucrative trade; they were ousting the Creole out of shingle making; they had taken over the sale of fabrics; they were underselling. All this, declared the press, was now called the Portuguese trade. And that *was* the rub! It was also claimed that the Portuguese who remained on the plantations were paid the highest wage – $28 per month to the $21 of the East Indian and even less for the Creoles. Thus the Creoles fumed the Portuguese were getting the fatted calf.

This growing animosity erupted in a series of riots during the nineteenth century. In May 1847 a mob of between 3,000-4,000 pillaged the Portuguese shops in New Amsterdam and again in 1848 when six shops suffered severe losses. These disturbances came on the heels of the Creoles' strike for better wages. They lashed out against the Portuguese strike-breakers, seeing them on the side of the planters. The most significant and disastrous of the riots was sparked off and instigated in February 1856 by James Sayers Orr known as the 'Angel Gabriel' – hence the 'Angel Gabriel Riots.' The riots broke in Georgetown and spread to the East Coast, Demerara and to the Essequibo. Portuguese shops and houses were sacked and for their losses the Portuguese submitted claims amounting to $286,752, for which they were granted $267,204. Although Governor Wodehouse classified the riots as 'a strife of Races', the Colonial Office viewed them in the more realistic light of economic jealousy. Khalill Mohammed investigating these riots pointed out in his thesis: 'The Negroes destroyed Portuguese property and not their persons' which supported his claim that the riots were seen by the Creoles as a means of lessening the economic clout of their rivals.

In March 1889 the 'Cent Bread' riots occurred – so called because a black lad took a "gill" (penny) bread instead of a cent bread from the Stabroek market stall of John Faria, whose assistant grabbed and hit him. When it was falsely rumoured that the boy had died the Creoles went on the rampage, what the *Daily Chronicle* euphemistically called 'a serious exhibition of temper on the part of the populace of the city.' Provision shops in Camp St, Bourda, Albuoystown, Alberttown, Meadowbank among others suffered grave losses. Special constables who were called out got their heads broken by both sides. The appearance of the Portuguese was like a red flag to a bull yet it was recorded that black men were hired by a Portuguese shopkeeper to protect his shop and it worked very well. A very exciting and detailed description of these riots was reported in the *Daily Chronicle* of 20, 21 March 1889.

THE PORTUGUESE AND THE CHURCH

Although in 1856 the 'Angel Gabriel' had castigated the Pope, the clergy and the nuns it was significant that the rioters had harmed neither the clergy nor the nuns. Undoubtedly, the Portuguese in B.G. were synonymous with the Catholic Church. Unquestionably, it was due to the Portuguese that the Catholic faith took firm root in the country. Because as a British colony the Church of England was the 'State-Church', the Portuguese had to make specific efforts to maintain their faith. In order to do so the Portuguese agitated to have their own priests administer to them. Since early 1841 when the Immigration Ordinance had been passed, over 2,500 Portuguese had arrived and had been located on the estates in all three counties. The Secretary of State, Lord Stanley, voiced his concern re the lack of priests and suggested asking the Portuguese government to send a priest to work among the emigrants. Stanley's cognisance of the need was probably due to the request of Rev W Bates, Vicar-General of the RC Church to the Court of Policy. The Courts were not at all willing to make financial provision for such a priest. At the end of 1841 with the increase of the Portuguese population the need became more acute. The local press stressed the need for Portuguese priests to be invited to B.G. in order 'to afford spiritual help to the Catholic population.' In October 1841, one priest, Irish not Portuguese, Rev Kelly was commissioned to work among the Portuguese in Essequibo. Bishop Clancy applied for four additional priests by the Combined Court did not see fit to vote their support. Governor Light considered this unjust, and observed that a refusal of the vote would have given the Portuguese government a good reason for opposing Madeiran emigration, had it been advisable to discontinue it at that time. Again in 1845 members of the Combined court were not opened to the motion for RC priests speaking the Portuguese language when there were not more than 4,000 Portuguese in the colony. Obviously, the Court saw no reason why the Portuguese should not learn to speak the Queen's English. It is reported in the annals of the Society for the Propagation of the Gospel that in areas such as Wakenaam and B.V. that the Portuguese, avid for religious instruction and services in their own language, attended Anglican chapels where some of the ministers spoke Portuguese.

Italian and Maltese priests who spoke Portuguese were finally introduced and Church records are replete with the missionary efforts of Fr Mosca, Casano, Lopristi, Emiliani, Mesini, Negri, Schembri, Poverelli, Casati and others who ministered to the Portuguese, and to their great contentment, preached in their language. To Fr Casati we owe the founding of the boys' orphanage at Plaisance. These priests gave instructions in Portuguese and held a special Sunday Mass in the Cathedral with ceremonies reminiscent of those to which they had been accustomed in Madeira. Consequently, there was a decided increase at services and the Sacraments.

In 1859 a Portuguese lady joined the Sisters at the Ursuline convent and in 1860 another Portuguese lady gave the first sum of $500 towards the building of a new church to be called the Portuguese Church where the Portuguese language only was to be spoken. In 1861 that new church – Sacred Heart Church, Main Street, was opened. The Bishop had forestalled the move for an independent church by legally securing the property, while the Jesuit Fathers were not at all happy with the suggestion of a separate school for Portuguese children, arguing quite rightly, that not all in the neighbourhood of the new church were Portuguese. Nor did they think it Catholic that the Portuguese were dealt with too much as a separate group.

Fr Walker criticised the Portuguese idea of Catholicity as 'what is done in Madeira which I hear is far from perfection in many ways.' But what was considered perfection in Catholic practice? The Portuguese had a long tradition of Catholicism and in Madeira it had acquired the earthy expression of the islanders – an exuberant type of religion not at all akin to the conservative, controlled Anglo-Saxon expression.

JOYFUL CELEBRATION OF RELIGIOUS FESTIVALS

The Madeirans, profoundly religious, celebrated their religious *festas* quite boisterously. They gained their greatest pleasure from participation in the many Church festivals, coming from all over the island to walk in procession – carrying life-size statues of the Saviour, the Virgin and the Saints shoulder-high, accompanied by the clergy, the military and bands of music. To round off the celebration gun shots were fired and fireworks exploded. One of their greatest feasts was the Feast of Nossa Senhora do Monte, in honour of the Mother of God whom the Madeirans claimed to have worked miracles. Like all other festivals it was preceded by a novena. Great enthusiasm and devotion greeted the statue of Our Lady of Fatima brought by Fr Patrick Moore to Sacred Heart Church in the 1940s. Thousands of people, not only Portuguese Catholics followed the statue in prayer throughout the country. Past students of Sacred Heart School would also remember the many processions in honour of Our Lady of Fatima. Other special *festas* in Madeira were the Feasts of St Peter, St John the Baptist, St Anthony and the Feast of Pentecost. The feast *par excellence* was the Feast of Christmas for which the Novens preparation was a unique one with the singing of the *Bemdita sajaes* at 4.30am before the Mass began.

In British Guiana these feasts were similarly celebrated. In 1858 the *Royal Gazette* reported the celebration of the Feast of Pentecost, at the Royal Hotel, Main Street. Coupled with the religious celebration was their charity to the poor; either preceding or concluding the occasion a dinner and a supply of clothing were given to the poor. This was not, the *Gazette* stated, 'the only occasion where the wealthier Portuguese have extended the hand of charity to the poor of the city.' After the distribution there was a procession to the RC church where Mass was celebrated.

The Portuguese also founded societies to assist the needy. Among these societies was the Portuguese Benevolent Society founded in the early 1870s – the aim of which was to help members when they had no other means of subsistance, to provide suitable burial expenses and to afford relief to widows and orphans. In 1887 this society changed its name to *Fraternidade Portugeza*. Another society the *Dona Maria Pia* was formed on the grounds that the earlier society was a failure. A member of the public disclaimed that the two societies were the same, writing to the press that they were 'as much strangers to each other as a Chinese is to a Barbadian'– a rather strange analogy!

A favourite feast among the societies was the Feast of St Anthony when the poor were specially remembered by the distribution of St Anthony's bread, a custom which continued in this country until recently. In the 19th century the Feast of St Peter was fittingly celebrated by the Portuguese fishermen around the Meadowbank and La Penitence areas. Small boats were carried in procession to the singing and accompaniment of bands. The new Meadowbank Church opened in December 1875 was the scene of many a festival. Bishop Etheridge recalled in his diary on 2 January 1876 that he had blessed a grand statue presented by a Portuguese after which it was carried in a very orderly procession two miles to the church. He also recorded in December that novena began in all Portuguese churches at 3.30am!

Another feast which delighted the young people was the Feast of St John the Baptist. One of the customs surrounding the feast was to break a fresh egg in a glass of water; the shape of the egg would determine one's destiny: a church, marriage; a ship, travel; a star, success. If it sank – disaster! Thus the Church of St John the Baptist at Plaisance, established in 1870, was especially beloved by the Portuguese. There are inumerable reports of novenas, Pontifical High Masses, processions, all capped with a dinner for the poor and that *sine qua non* of the celebrations – fireworks.

In 1858 Fr Sherlock, an English Jesuit, had written of his parishioners in Georgetown:

> The Portuguese are hardworking, sober, industrious people . . . They have entirely supplanted the old creole population and in Georgetown and New Amsterdam there are many of them wholesale merchants rivalling the English even. Many of them are very wealthy. At Georgetown our congregation is more substantial than any I know in England.

Over the years their adherence to their faith grew. The Portuguese newspaper, *A Uniao Portugueza,* noted in 1890: 'Their love for their church is plainly seen in their self-denial and their strict observance of feasts, fasts and days of obligation.'

CULTURAL INFLUENCE

The Portuguese were not only involved with their religious celebrations. Many secular occasions were marked by concerts by the Portuguese bands, by dramatic plays, balls at the Assembly Rooms and parades. Love for music and dancing was an inherited trait from their island home and they made use of every occasion to display their art. On the fourth centenary of the discovery of the sea route to India by Vasco Da Gama, the Portuguese explorer, the Portuguese marked the occasion by gala and lavish festivities and illuminations of their business houses and private homes. There were bicycle parades and concerts at which the leading Portuguese band, *Primeiro do Dezembro* entertained.

The Portuguese community was notified of all these occasions in a number of newspapers published by and for them. The latter part of the 19th century saw a spate of such newspapers: *The Watchman* (1871) was published in Portuguese and English by C K Jardine. It was extremely critical of government policies but in its middle page noted the dates and times of feasts and reported on their solemnities; *A União Portugueza, O Voz Portuguez* and *Chronica Semanal* featured during the 1890s. The *Chronica Semanal* – Commercial, Politico, Noticioso e Religioso, was published every Saturday by P M Valladares and carried innumerable advertisements of the leading Portuguese businesses as well as articles on the various celebrations, both sacred and secular.

In order to preserve the language which later died out private schools teaching Portuguese were opened. Although this was somewhat frowned upon by others in the society and were eventually scrapped, today it is a great pity that the descendants of the Portuguese in Guyana, with very few exceptions, can no longer speak nor understand their language. This lacuna has been mostly responsible for the lack of awareness and understanding of the rich culture of the Portuguese which our nineteenth century ancestors in British Guiana cherished and fostered and shared.

Arrival of Portuguese

On 3 May 1935, the 'Louisa Baillie' docked in the Demerara River bringing in her hold the first 40 Madeirans who were imported as agricultural labourers to British Guiana. From a knowledge of the history of the Madeirenses and their beautiful Atlantic island, one learns that times were hard in Madeira due to the failure of both the sugar and the vine crops. Added to these two problems the Madeiran did not wish to become involved in the civil war then being carried on in Portugal. He came to British Guiana as industrious labour, eager and willing to make good, indeed much too willing and too eager and fell prey to sickness and death. The rather exaggerated account given by Governor Henry Light of Portuguese mortality in the 1840's led the British Government to proclaim a stoppage of the Madeirans, seeing them 'as quite unsuitable to the climate of British Guiana.'

Not only were the authorities in British Guiana and London against Madeiran emigration but so too those in Madeira who viewed the loss of their people with a rather jaundiced eye, proclaiming that 'these unfortunates were subject to a fate similar to that of black slaves in other times'. Yet it was agreed that many returned bringing money which helped to support both their families and their church, thus tempting others to set out for Demerara and try their luck.

Arrival of Portuguese from Madeira – 3 May 1835
PORT OF DEMERARY
3 May – Louisa Baillie, Wildgoos, London and Madeira – 78 days
'By the Louisa Baillie – WILDGOOS, arrived in the river yesterday(?) from London via Madeira, forty of the peasantry of that island have been imported as agricultural labourers; twenty of them are engaged to James H Albouy, Esq, and the other twenty to R G Butts, Esq.

The competency of these Islanders to perform the work expected of them is a matter of great importance to ascertain, as if the experiment is successful, it is calculated that of the hundred and twenty thousand inhabitants of Madeira, at least a tithe would be willing to emigrate.'

(Editorial in *The Royal Gazette,* Thursday, 5 May, 1835)

The Madeiran Immigrants seen as setting an example of field labour to the negroes

'They are very industrious and as yet, have given great satisfaction to their employers. They work in the field and bear the heat of the sun as well as the Negro. The food which they receive (several Potatoes, Yams and Plantains mixed up with salt fish), is the same as what they have been accustomed to all their lives. They drink no Spirits. It is understood that a considerable number of these valued Labourers can be procured at Madeira. Several Proprietors have already agreed with Masters of Merchant Vessels to stop at Madeira on their voyage out here and to bring Madeira Labourers to this colony. I am in hopes that this measure will prove of the greatest advantage to British Guiana. The apprenticed Labourer will witness a number of free men, working willingly and cheerfully, on the same Estate with himself and contented with a very moderate hire. The character of the Free Labourer cannot but be raised in his own estimation, and in that of the Negroes generally when they witness free White Men willingly submit to the same employment.'

(J Carmichael Smyth to Earl of Aberdeen, 25 May 1835)

Reasons for Portuguese Mortality

'Of the industry of these people we have had satisfactory proof; their eagerness to reap the advantage of their industry has made them imprudently laborious; unused to sickness they would neither be persuaded to precaution, nor take the remedies either of food or medicine necessary for recovery from sickness; then came despondency and death.'

(Sir Henry Light to Lord Stanley, No 55, 22 November 1841)

' . . . have gorged themselves with ripe and unripe fruit, sleep at night on the grass, improperly expose themselves in the sun, refuse to take medicine . . . '

'Out of 41, 37 required active Treatment for fever with excessive debility, for dropsy consequent on fever, for dysentry and diarrhoea.'

(Monthly Returns of Portuguese Emigrants – enclosures in Light to Stanley, 22 November 1841)

Expressions of Joy by Portuguese on Arrival in Demerara. 1842

. . . In no instance has any death taken place or sickness occurred during the passage of any immigrant vessel hither, neither has there been occasion, on their arrival, to find fault with or condemn the accommodations on provisions on board for the use of the (immigrants) emigrants, who on landing appeared almost invariably in good spirits, and well pleased with their reception and the appearance of the country.

This expression of satisfaction has been particularly remarkable with regard to the Portuguese emigrants from Madeira, who generally commence dancing and singing the moment the vessels come to anchor, and on leaving the ship not unfrequently caress and embrace the sailors, in token of gratitude for having brought them safely; and on their arrival at the depot on Plantation Poaderayen they begin to tune their guitars, and a general dance follows which they keep up for hours.

These people have been all comfortably located, the greater portion of them in the vicinity of Georgetown; Mr James, the opulent proprietor of plantation Houston, having taken the whole party of one of the last vessels, amounting to 81, including women and children, several of whom I have since seen, and they expressed themselves contented and happy in their situations . . .

(Mr James Hackett to Governor Henry Light, enc in no. 4, 5 July 1841. *Relative to the West Indies. British Guiana 1841-2* (London, 1842)).

Stoppage of Madeirans

The return of the Portuguese emigrants from Madeira presents a melancholy contrast, and prove beyond a doubt that, before they can be acclimatised, an immense mortality and sickness must take place among them.

I have the honour to transmit copy of letter from Stipendary Magistrate Allen from the Arabian coast, Essequibo, an extract from Mr Ball, and copies of letter from Mr Strutt to the Government Secretary and to the Sheriff of Berbice on the state of these emigrants.

It appears, from the general returns of deaths in the three counties, 281 have died since the first arrival in February last out of 3,000 and upwards, and even this statement cannot include those who have been induced to give their labour to woodcutters in the rivers, Demerara and its tributary creeks.

That many will be acclimatised there is no doubt; but I consider that it was neither advantagous to the colony to incur such great expense, nor according to the dictates of humanity to induce ignorant people to come to a climate which must be fatal to so large a proportion of their number.

I, therefore, proposed at once to the Court of Policy to stop the introduction of labourers from Madeira, as soon as it conveniently could be done . . .

(Governor Henry Light to Lord Stanley, No 157, 22 November 1841)

Portuguese Work Satisfactorily

My Lord,

I have the honour to transmit the returns of the Stipendary Magistrates for the month of November, with summary by Mr Wolsely; also separate returns of the Coolies, Portuguese emigrants, Sierra Leone emigrants and captured Africans. The Coolies, and the two last-mentioned emigrants, continue almost without a casuality.

The deaths among the Portuguese are not quite so numerous; and, on examination of the causes of death, the diseases are not generally from the effects of climate.

I believe, notwithstanding the mortality amongst the Portuguese, that they feel their condition ameliorated by coming to this Colony; and animated by the knowledge they have of the facility of making money by their industry, they in no way despond: all who do work give satisfaciton to their employers. [In Mr Wolseley's summary, allusion is made to observations by Mr Brittain, that some of the employers charge high for cottages, when the occupants do not work for the estates.

If these charges mare made and enforced, unless a mutual agreement has been sanctioned by the Stipendary Magistrate, they are illegal, and, whenever complained of, invariably redressed. Mr Brittain will be called on to give further explanation . . .]

(Governor Henry Light to Lord Stanley, No 177, 26 December 1841)

Stoppage approved by Colonial Secetary

Downing Street
February 17, 1841

Sir,

I have received your Despatch of the 22nd November, No 157, transmitting the returns of the state of the Coolies, the captured Africans, the emigrants from Sierra Leone, and of the Portuguese emigrants from Madeira.

I have perused with much concern your account, and also the statements which accompany your Despatch, relative to the Portuguese emigrants from Madeira.

It is clear that this description of labourers is quite unsuited to the climate of British Guiana, and I approve therefore of the steps which you have taken for preventing any more being sent to the colony from Madeira at the public expense.

With respect to the African immigrants, the accounts are of a most satisfactory nature, and there appears every reason to expect that they will become a valuable acquisition to the colony.

(Lord Stanley to Governor Henry Light, No 56, 17 February 1842)

Madeira's Views on Emigration – Pro and Con

It was obvious from accounts in the Madeira press that there were many strong objections to the Madeirans leaving the island for Demerara. The smaller the country there was an even greater need to hold the population. It was also obvious that the poor economic conditions of the island had necessitated the exodus, but fears were voiced that the emigrants would meet a similar fate to those of the blacks in British Guiana. Yet it was conceded that quite a few *Demeraristas* (as the Madeirans who went to Demerara were called) returned with sufficient wealth to be able to support their families and their church, thus tempting others to try their luck in the much publicised 'El Dorado'.

'O Defensor', No 105 Saturday 1st January 1842
The Defender, Friday 31st December 1841

Here we are at the end of 1841, a year that will be well remembered by the Madeirans as that from which will date the last period of their decadence – if appropriate legislation doesn't come soon to save them. This year is noteworthy for Madeira for the large emigration that took place to B.G. as a consequence of the invitation that was made to peasants and other workers, an invitation that would not have been accepted if the hunger and misery, necessary consequences of the stagnation of our economy had not obliged them to. The measles also came to decimate our population and its ill effects especially among the poorest classes have been and still are very great.

We leave the, '1841' without bitterness, but also without hope that 1842 will be more favourable to us let us hope that we are wrong.

From 'O Defensor' No 112 Saturday 19 February 1842
Demerara:

1. We have at hand a report made for the Governor of that colony by a commission charged with the study of the plantations which had Madeirans working on. The commision laments that the climate has killed more than a ¼ of them, which it largely attributes to their having arrived in the worst season of the year. It found that in some plantations they were not well treated but in the majority of cases they were. The commission found that the greatest need of the labourers was the lack of priests to administer the comforts of their religion.

In spite of the caution with which the commission expresses itself, it can be inferred that the mortality among the emigrants has been considerable so much so that it is doubtful if more Colonists will be sent there from this island.

1. 'O Defensor' No 106 Saturday 8 January 1842
Foreign News
Demerera

The Journal of Commerce of the 6th of last month says that business in Demerara was very poor, there is little money and the value of property is minimal. Steam ploughs have been introduced.

'As Novidades' Thursday 6 September, 1866
To Demerara:

On the 15th of September next, the Portuguese pinnace 'Greyhound' will sail without fail to the above mentioned port. This ship is about to arrive from Lisbon.

Those desirous of sailing on board this ship should contact the charter João de Freitas Martins in the R dos Tanoeiros in order to give in their name and to present their documents as soon as possible in order to obtain a passport in time.

Funchal 30 August, 1866

Elucidano Madeirense
A work commissioned by the General Council of the district destined to commemorate the fifth centenary of the discovery of Madeira Volume 1 A-1 (Funchal Esperanca Printers 1921).

Emigration: (346)

Emigration to Demerara and the English West Indian Colonies seems only to have begun on a large scale around 1840. In 1841 the number of emigrants rose to 4045 in 1846 to 4945, in 1847 to 4720 and in 1853 to 3060. The English Government paid the passages of those emigrants, because of the lack of manpower in those Colonies. In 1847 a Portuguese warship was stationed in our waters in order to help the local authorities repress clandestine emigration.

Of the thousands of Madeirans who went to B.G. and the other English Colonies in search of wealth, some were lucky and their decendants still live in those countries as well as amongst us. The Demerarista who at the cost of back breaking work and all sorts of hardships, succeeded in amassing capital did not as a rule forget the land of his birth and it was here that he likes to come to spend the rest of his life surrounded by the comforts that he had not been accustomed to in his youth. It was he who spent the most in his parish on the feasts of 'Our Lord', feasts in which there was always a lot of fireworks, which are very pleasing to simple people of our island.

FROM THE *DIARIO DE NOTICIAS* – SPECIAL SUPPLEMENT ON THE CONGRESS OF PORTUGUESE COMMUNITIES

The Emigration that has taken place recently, has only taken place among incautious persons who take the risk of going as a result of flattering promises of wealth which are never realised, to seek greater fortune in those unknown countries. Demerara to where there has been a large emigration is an English possession, its climate being so hot and unhealthy that it puts an end to the existence of the majority of emigrants who go there; these unfortunates are subject to a most cruel fate similar to that of black slaves in other times; particularly painful are the circumstances of some married couples as their partners may be contracted to different proprietors and be there obliged to live far from each other.

It is certain, however, that of the hundreds of persons who have left Madeira some have returned with money, whilst others come to tempt more Colonists. It is known that the Colonial Government of Demerara has chartered two boats to bring Colonists, one from Madeira the other from Sierra Leone (Adapted from Domingos Olavo Correa de Azevedo – Administrator of Funchal – year 1841).

The Demerarista who returned wealthy at the cost of arduous work not only bought land in his home area, but offered religious feasts, in his parish in honour of the Lord, feasts with many fireworks and orchestras. His neighbours seeing their companion formerly as poor as he, rich owner of lands, lost his last doubts. Why not leave and try his luck. The success of the Demerarista and its consequences were identical to those of the 'Mineiros' of Portugal when they returned. Let us analyse some statistics.

An issued passport can cover more than one person in a family.

In a period of 13 years 7445 passports were issued. The number of persons, who actually left during this time can be calculated at 2 or 3 times the number of passports.

Years	Passport Issued	Total Emigrants
1853	545	1878
1854	755	1976
1855	909	2067

In 1857 2230 passports were issued.

Destination of Madeirans for Emigration:

Years	Demerara	Brasil	USA	South America	West Indies	Europe	Africa	India
1853	367	85	33	1	55	–	3	–
1854	436	143	42	8	116	1	4	–
1855	325	460	6	–	103	6	4	2
Total	1128	688	81	9	274	7	11	2

Emigration:

Years	Demerara
1858	1604
1859	918
1860	585
1861	276
1862	300

Life in the island was difficult. Let us see what people were saying about it then.

'Emigration to Demerara and Trinidad has not ceased up to now 1847 – Counsellor Jose Silvestre Ribeiro'.

'It is a custom for people to complain all the time. Those of this island although they have many reasons for complaining are not the worst off in this world. As bad as the situation is here it is not desperate. One obstacle is the geological structure of the island. When wine was expensive the least expensive land produced the most, then the peasants could face up to their expenses – another obstacle that worsened this state of affairs is the lack of irrigation water . . . now the supply of water is less . . . but worst of all for the peasant which kills him with hunger at home or compels him to emigrate and die of pests is the system of landownership which suffers from the malign influences of feudalism (adapted from Counsellor José S Ribeiro).

Weighing the cane at the factory

Cutting sugar cane

The Sugar Cane Industry: Madeira (From *Impressions of Madeira in the Past* by Prof Luis de Sousa Melo and Susan E Farrow)

Portuguese in Business

' . . . By small gains and great economy'

Not 10 years after their arrival the Portuguese moved into the huckster trade, supplying the plantation workers with basic supplies. By 1843, the Portuguese were importing their own goods from Madeira, especially their Madeira wines which they missed and for which their island was famed. The local press praised their 'sagacity, daring and ambition'. The next step was the establishment of shops and these, provision as well as spirit shops, mushroomed in the country as well as in the city. As their commercial progress and success grew so did creole jealousy and animosity, climaxing in the 1856 Portuguese riots which the *Daily Chronicle* writing on the 31st Anniversary called a misnomer as it was not the Portuguese who rioted. Despite the set back with the heavy loss of property, the Portuguese continued to expand their business, in quantity and variety of goods as the enclosed advertisements illustrate.

Other writers on the Portuguese business expertise viewed them merely as owners of salt goods and rum shops. Not so – the Portuguese were more enterprising than that; they moved into every type of business – hotels, ice-houses, hardware stores, mining, wood-cutting, commission agents, cocoa and chocolate industry, wicker work and, last but not least, the production of cassava and plantain flour and corn meal.

The few Portuguese of the mid 20th century continued to be men of business acumen and enterprise as is evidenced in Banks DIH (expansion of the Demerara Ice House of the D'Aguiar Bros) and John Fernandes, Ltd which business is a long-standing one, boasting of an earlier Joffer Coal industry and continuing as the leading shipping agents of Guyana. J P Santos and Co Ltd, whose founder was a well-known philanthropist of his day, is soon to celebrate its 100th Anniversary in 1986.

The Firm of Central Garage established in 1915, still continues under Mr John Simon De Freitas.

Portuguese Move Into Huckster Trade in 1840s

'Portuguese immigrants, as hucksters, nearly monopolise the country traffic. Cotton goods are most in demand. The demand for salt provisions, rice, etc., and malt liquours is considerable.'

(Encl No 4 in No 29 Light to Lord Russell, 21 August 1841)

First Import of Goods by Portuguese – 1843

Within the last few days, a brigantine called the ZARGO has arrived in our river from Madeira, under circumstances which seem likely to lead to great future changes in the commercial history of this country.

The vessel, which was of small size, had been chartered, for the large sum of $1900 (£380) by a couple of Portuguese, on their own account, and that of some of their fellow-countrymen, who had all within a very few years emigrated to this colony in a state of most complete poverty, and who after trafficking for a short time as the keepers of petty shops, had returned to their own country for the purpose of laying in a large assortment of goods as importers to the Demerary market. The cargo . . . consists of wines, esculents of various sorts, and a quantity of fancy articles . . .

The rapid growth of the fortunes of these people now, as it would seem about to enter our markets as general merchants and importers, is attributable, in a great measure, to the assistance they received from many mercantile firms of between 4 and 5 years back, after the passing of the measure of the emancipation. To explain this, it is necessary to state a certain object which our commercial houses of that day, and many other influential parties in the Colony had in view. A great part of the small retail or huckster trade, as it is called, was at that time in the hands of a large number of our native population, the members of which either kept little shops in the towns, or travelled about the country with packages of goods for sale to the different estates, the villages on which, inhabited by the labourers, are, in most instances remote from each other. It was thought that could these traffickers, many of whom having been brought up to no other calling were fit for no other, be thrown out of their old employment by successful competition, the necessary consequence would be that they must all be driven into the field to earn their livelihood. To a certain extent, partially, though far from uniformly, this expectation was answered. By the coalition that had been entered into between the Portuguese and those whom we have mentioned, these foreigners, whose savings had not then amounted to enough to raise them from a condition of the most abject misery, and many of whom had shortly before arrived in the colony as indented laborers, –an occupation which they took the first opportunity of giving up in disgust, – were entrusted in the first instance with goods, on the easiest of terms of credit, to carry about the country and to dispose of the estates' people; while their native rivals were favoured with no credit at all, or a very stringent one. On these advantageous terms, the Portuguese pedlars soon drove the natives engaged in the same line, though entirely off the field, not exactly into it, as was anticipated. Numbers of the ejected flocked into the towns, and have remained in them ever since, earning their subsistence in a precarious, and not always a very commendable way. The Portuguese, however, had not yet completely defeated their competitors. They had bested them on the road, and in the rural districts; to these latter still remained the command of the small settled trade in the towns. But the strangers had already gained a great advantage; they had derived, moreover, some profit from their new enterprise. The same parties, who had formerly assisted them, still lent them a helping hand to further deeds: little imagining that the day would ever come when the poor and humble dependent would think of exaulting himself to the same pitch as the opulent and haughty patron. Credit had already been made easy to the Portuguese and when they became purchaser in the warehouses of the merchants, it was found that to start shops of their own, Portuguese money went further than any other. What was the consequence? It followed almost as rapidly as it may be told.

The Portuguese became the monopolists of the whole retail trade of the country; for they immediately undersold, and the reason is not to be wondered at, everybody else in the same way of business as themselves. These two causes have been the peculiar secrets of their eminent and most remarkable success. A few short years have glided by, and lo! we behold them the posessors of thousands, and begining to take their stand, side by side, on an equality, with the great importing merchants of the country. The small domestic trade they have already made their own;

they are now about to enter upon the wider path of foreign commerce; with what success events will show. The attempts proves that they are not destitute either of sagacity, daring, or ambition.

(*The Royal Gazette*, 3 October 1843)

The number of shops in the district affords evidence of considerable internal traffic; many new ones have been opened by the Portuguese during the last six months, who seem to be gradually supplanting every other description of petty trader.

It frequently happens that a shop which is found unprofitable, and has been relinquished by the former owner, a European or Creole, is rented or purchased by a Portuguese, whose activity and address seem at once to attract custom, and his superior industry and economy enable him to turn to advantage a position which the more expensive and indolent habits of his predecessor rendered profitless.

(Stipendiary Magistrate William Carbery of West Coast Essequibo, June 1845)

Petition of Manuel Pereira

Manuel Pereira – emigrated in 1841, completed 3 year indenture, managed a shop with wife on Leguan for a year then opened a shop in Alberttown in late 1845.

MINUTES OF THE COURT OF POLICY 20 January, 1847

To his Excellency Henry Light Esquire Governor and Commander-in-Chief in and over the Colony of British Guiana. Vice Admiral and ordinary of the same and to the Honourable the Court of Policy of the said colony.

The Humble Petition of Manuel Pereira a Portuguese Emigrant lately residing in Alberttown.

Respectfully sheweth

That about five years ago your petitioner emigrated from his native country to the Colony of British Guiana with the prospect as it was held out to him, that by honest industry and economy, he would be able to gain, not only a lively hood for himself and family, but as indeed if afterwards proved to save a portion of his earnings.

That your petitioner and his wife were field labourers on Plantation Housten during the first six months and subsequently in Leguan during two and a half years.

That your petitioner with the savings of the joint labour of himself and his wife, commenced business as a shopkeeper, first on Leguan, and toward the latter part of last year, he established himself as such in Alberttown taking out his license and to the best of his knowledge, complying with every necessary formality and conducting himself as a quiet citizen.

That on or about the 1st of April last in the evening your petitioner was, in his own house, cruelly assailed by an infuriated mob – as he was entirely without protection, and as neither remonstrance nor solicitations were of any avail, your petitioner's wares, merchandise, and even cash amounting to upwards of five hundred dollars not the value of a cent excepted – because a prey to the capacity of a tumultous populace, against which he has committed no other offense, than coming to this country and gaining an honest lively hood, which the assailants maintained was taking the bread out of their mouths.

That your petitioner now being threatened with having the house pulled down and with violence to his person, was forced to escape which he did, suffering a severe beating as he forced his way through the crowds, carrying with him nothing but the clothes he had on his person at the time.

That the wife of your petitioner in escaping with her infant of three months old in her arms, received a violent blow from a heavy stick in the lower part of her stomach in consequence of which she has been unable to work and ever since suffered from an infirmity which the Doctors in the Colonial Hospital have tried in vain to cure, but recommend her to return to Madeira as her only chance of a restoration of health.

That your petitioner is extremely anxious to return to Madeira as the only refuge for his sick wife, but has neither the means of defraying the expenses nor anything to subsist upon there.

That your petitioner believes it to be the just and Liberal practice of a British Legislature in isolated cases of this kind to indemnify the sufferer who sustains losses through public riots on the equitable ground that as a taxpayer, if for no other reason he was entitled to the protection of his person and property by the police towards the maintenance of whom he was a contributor.

That should your Excellency and your Honourable Court in your justice and wisdom consider the hardships of your petitioner deserving a compensation for his losses and sufferings, great confidence and gratitude would naturally be established among all his countrymen whilst it would at the same time destroy one at least of the malicious motives any similar rioters in future might have in view namely that of ruining the intended victim.

That your petitioner most humbly and most earnestly prays that your Excellency and your Honourable Court will be pleased to take the aforesaid circumstances into your favourable, just and charitable consideration and indemnify your petitioner for the severe losses he has sustained and your petitioner as in duty bound will ever pray.

Demerara 29th December 1846

his
Manuel ——┼—— Pereira
mark

Witness John Evangelist.

The Colonist Comments on the Commercial Progress of Portuguese

The Madeirans, it is true, have taken the trade out of the hands of the Creoles, but that is less the misfortune than the fault of the natives. They cannot compete with their rivals, because they are generally deficient in that industry, economy and perseverance which characterise the exertions of the Portuguese. It is no common praise to a race who came here scarce 10 years ago destitute and penniless, that, in many instances, they are now wealthy merchants, forming the intermediate link between the greats importing firms and the retail shops. They have turned their industry into every available channel and in every instance with marked success. They have broken down the monopolies and materially cheapened the rate of living, and in that they have benefitted the colony to an incredible extent.

(*The Colonist*, 5 March 1852)

The Colonist of British Guiana March 19, 1855

'The Portuguese have taken the retail provision trade out of the hands of the merchants, and they are now entering largely into the boot and shoe trade. While the ambulating merchants of the pavements can produce anything, from a wedding ring to a coffin handle, from their basket of odds and ends. These boys are capital customers to the merchants and help to pass off the heavy stock. The trade is certainly on the increase, for there is scarcely a store that has not one or two hangers-on of this description. That it is profitable is clear from the fact that long ere the exceptionable ROGERS has reaped to the glories of the mental soil, our young friends become partners in some flourishing shop, and can throw in their lot with the master as independently as the best. We regret that these really enterprising people have not turned their attention more to provision grounds, seeing that on every estate they could have abundance of ground for the asking, and that with their industrious habits, they could easily cultivate it in their own hours, without in any way interfering with the work of the plantation. They have succeeded in establishing the coal business as a lucrative trade, and in cutting out the creoles in shingle making, and as the retail shops are in their hands, it would be a capital speculation for any shopkeeper to supply himself constantly with ground provisions to sell in his shop.

The colony's retail trade is

. . . almost entirely in the hands of a class of persons who are in no way akin to the British tradesman . . . they are intensely practical. By habits of frugality and self-denial – perhaps also by other means – habits in which they altogether surpass their competitors, they have got almost all the retail trade into their own hands, and they are wise enough to see that by combination they can quickly become wealthy, whilst by competition they may remain petty shopkeepers for life.

There is no chance of finding goods cheaper in one Portuguese shop than another, the prices are the same in all.

(*The Creole,* 13 June 1873)

A. A. D'Andrade offers for Sale

THE CARGO
of the
Brigt. "Clio" from Lisbon in 25 days

All in Prime Order and at Reasonable Rates

21 Bags CORKS	10½ Barrels ALBACORE
5 Crates GOGLETS	6046 Bundles ONIONS
112 Barrels Coarse SALT	200 Barrels POTATOES
260 Pairs Strings GARLIC	75 Boxes VERMICELLI
30 Kents OLIVES	75 Boxes MACARONI

GENT'S WIDE ELASTIC SIDE BOOTS

5 Bags ALMONDS

300 Bags Black Eye PEASE		30 Bags WALNUTS	
150 Boxes		4 Barrels LAMP OIL	
150½ do	FIGS	1800 Tins BLACKING	
150¼ do		21 Dozen BASINS	
150 Boxes		100 Tins Preserved FRUITS	
150½ do	RAISINS	150 Ditto Tomato SAUCE	
150¼ do			

Robb's Town, Water St., 13 November 1865

(*GUIANA Times,* 21 November 1865)

ADVERTISEMENT
John Martins
offers for Sale
Ex "Funchal" from Madeira
A Great Quantity
of
WICKER WORK
such as

LARGE ARM CHAIRS
Small Arm Chairs for Children
Large SOFAS
Small Sofas for Children
At reasonable rates, at his store in Water Street next to Messrs
BROWNE, GILBERT AND CO
Lot No 14 Demerara, Feb 26 1869

(*The Colonist* Tues, 2nd March, 1869)

THE UNDERSIGNED
offers for Sale
Ex brig 'Funchal' from Madeira

15 BAGS Corks, Wine, Soda and Porter

28 Large Bags BEANS

10 tins 1 Gallon each HONEY

234 strings GARLIC

1 Quater Cask Superior MADEIRA WINE
   none of this Colony equal

   Also in Bond

25 Qtrs casks Madeira New WINE   2 H hds Madeira New Wine

Calisto José Nunes, Water Street. 25th Feb. 1869

(*The Colonist.* Tues 2 March, 1869)

J.A. Perreira – The White Cocoanut Tree – selling celebrated brands of Brandys, Wines, Liqueur and Malt Liquors. Old Rum (11 years old) Madeira – 8 years. Port, Sherry, Cherry Brandy, Gin, Whiskey

Old Men and Young Friends at Christmas meet,
 Christmas to all 'tis a treat;
  While the bough bend
  To the cocoanut send
And obtain Ladies your sweets –
Of Curacoa, Noyeau, Cordial and Shrub
Falernum v.o. Rum, and ach! That's the rub.
December 20, 1871

(*The Watchman,* 6 January 1872)

The Watchman Friday November 10, 1876
EDITORIAL:

The Portuguese shopkeepers are hardly dealt with! They are virtually the collectors of a large portion of the revenue. They sacrifice every comfort and put up with all sorts of insults to catch the pennies of the people. They set up late to accomodate everybody, and they rise early to meet their customers to whom they are so civil and obliging. From them the poor can always get an extra trifle if they have not the extra penny. The people prefer to buy from them than from creoles, who must fail in that line. In selling, they never, never merely give balance of weight which alone the law demands or expects. They always give down weight. We call the Public to witness and we hearby declare to the fact tried by ourselves over and over. Now, if they give more than the law demands, a downweight and an overfull measure and if the people have never had any shopkeepers up for shortweight, this ought to weigh with the Magistrates when these busy people are pounced upon by the gentlemen commissaries and their weights are carried far away on suspicion, causing them to forego the uses of their weights, stopping their business, preventing them from making up their sales so as to pay the merchant who had advanced the colony the duty on the article, depending upon the return of these poor sellers. This is a serious damage to hard working people, and this by very nice and educated gentlemen. Then if they get a sharp and brisk young lawyer to defend them, they are fined the maximum as if thro' spite, whilst the one who employs no counsel is fined the very minimum of the law, as if to say: 'I shall prevent the Portuguese from employing you'. Then again, no allowance is made for the corrosion of weight, cleaning, wear and waste of the metal, but these everlasting weights must always balance with the idling one at the office in Georgetown.

New Ice House

His Excellency the Governor expected to pay an unofficial visit of inspection to the New Ice House . . . The New Ice House, as is generally, has been erected under the supervision of the Colonial Civil Engineer's Department, from plans furnished by Mr C Castellani. Mr Castellani has attained considerable notoriety as a local architect, his private commissions comprising the design for the towers of the Brick Dam Police Station, residence of the Solicitor General, the facade of Sacred Heart Church, the new Alms House, The R C Cathedral, The Tower Hotel, etc. With respect to the Ice House however, the designs were drawn by Mr Castellani in the ordinary course of departmental business. The erection being now complete, the public have ample opportunity of judging as to the character of the work. The general contract was intrusted to the Demerara Wood Working Co, whose manager, Mr David Smith has directed the progress of the work to the satisfaction of the Civil Engineer's Department. Considering that only four months in all has been occupied in the demolition of the old Establishment and the erection of the new one, the contractors are entitled to praise for the manner in which they have executed the task allotted to them. The ground floor will be used as an ordinary public bar room. On the windward side is a verandah, which will be available as a cool lounging place for the patrons of the establishment. At each of the four corners of the room, has been placed a little 'snuggery' affording to those who desire in the privacy which is impossible at the open bar. The latter which is of pine wood, and will be surmounted by a marble top, is 28 feet long, and stands out a distance of 15 feet from the wall. The marble top is on its way to the colony from the US. The bar-room floor is of

concrete. Access is obtained to the upper rooms by means of two grand staircases of pitch pine. The second story, as it now stands, consists of a spacious hall, with an arcade running round it. It is intended to divide the hall into two sections, and in the northern one, that to the windward, will be placed two large billiard tables. The other section will be as a select bar and refreshment room. The hass is 30 feet wide, exclusive of tea galleries, which are 10 feet in width, 50 feet long; and 18 feet in height. Including the galleries its area will be about 70 feet by 50 feet. It is lighted at the sides by 72 windows, with semi-circular heads, and having jalousies at the top and bottom. Each window has a 'triple sash' containing nine glass panes in rows of three each, and each fitted with a novel mechanical arrangement by which three sashes can be opened or shut simultaneously. There are 18 'arches' opening from the hall into the arcades, and if in course of time it be found necessary, what is now a gallery will be shut off into 18 little rooms. The sloping ceiling of the gallery is painted in sky-blue, similar to the ceiling of the main room, the roof of which is raised about 6 feet above that of the gallery and is lighted by 18 semi-circular windows corresponding with the arches beneath. The bar, which it is proposed to place at the southern extremity of the hall, will form the division between the public part and the apartments for the use of the staff of the establishment. The intention is to make this bar in three sections; the centre part, which will be semi-circular in shape, will be used for serving out liquors, and the side sections for serving warm dinners, pastry etc. Behind the bar is a large lattice work screen, which serves to shield from observation those engaged in culinary and other operations. The kitchen is situated at the south-west corner and has a raised floor constructed of brick. Here a large cooking stove has been placed, manufactured by Leibrandt and McDowell Stove Company, Philadelphia. The roof is of slate. A road will skirt the exterior of the whole building, with four large bridges leading to the principal throughfares in the neighbourhood. The general framework of the building has been constructed of green heart timber. His Excellency's visit today is not intended as the opening of the place. Much yet remains to be done in the interior, but when all the fittings and furnishings have been placed in position it will be found that a place of public resort and convenience has been provided which will stand unequalled in the West Indies. The lessee, Senhor Fernandes, has acted wisely in making the establishment something more than a mere drinking saloon, and when all appliances which have been provided for are in full swing, we may expect the project will meet with the hearty approval of the public.

(*The Daily Chronicle* Fri 4 August, 1882)

THE PORTUGESE PAWNBROKING CO LTD

Founded 1886

One of the Oldest Pawnbroking concerns in British Guiana

16 ROBB & HINCKS ST.
GEORGETOWN, B.G.

General Merchants - Jewellers - Importers Specialising in Loans on Pledges

Gold, Diamond, Silver, Electroplated ware & Wrist Watches

Re 'Portuguese' Riots

'The Angel Gabriel has a good deal to answer for. We do not, it may be desirable to state, refer to any scriptual celebrity; but to one John Sayers Orr, a creole of this colony, who assumed the name as one of many aliases. He was mainly instrumental in creating what are commonly called the Portuguese riots, which took place thirty-one years ago today, on Friday the 18th of February, 1856. The circumstances are called to mind by a letter appearing in our last issue wherein 'Teneriffe' appositely asked whether it is not time the riots were more accurately described than by qualifying them with the prefix of the word Portuguese. We plead guilty to the soft impeachment which is implied in the communication of our Friend From the Canaries; and henceforward we will improve our almanack by a more accurate description of the events which made this day memorable in the year '56. Thirty-one years is a pretty long period in the history of such a colony as British Guiana, and covers more than half the space which has elapsed since the union of the three counties took place. It may not therefore, be without interest if we take a peep into the past, and revive the recollections of some of our readers, while collecting some of the popular impressions which exist as to the Portuguese riots. One of these days, when the British Guiana Antiquarian Society exists, and when an increasingly intelligent people take a more intelligent interest in the land in which they live, these chronicles of olden times will probably be placed on record in some more convenient form than the files of the colonial newspapers, where the information is necessarily incomplete and infragmentary in character – still enough is to be found in the diminutive columns of these organs of editorial personality and public opinion – for the former too often predominated over the latter – to give some of idea of the damage which was done and of the serious consequences which were threatened at the time. It seems that the Angel Gabriel, otherwise John Sayers Orr, as aforesaid, after creating riots in New York, Greenock and Glasgow by fanatical speeches against the Roman Catholic Church, returned to his native country to continue his discreditable career. One of our journalistic predecessors states that he 'created a considerable amount of bad feeling amongst the black population of the city by his inflammatary speeches against what he terms the abuses and vices of the Roman Catholic Church.' At a time when there was some disaffection among a portion of the black people at what they considered to be Favouritism shown by Governor Wodehouse to the Portuguese, the excited language of the angel Gabriel easily took hold upon popular superstition and ignorance. In the words of a contemporary 'the latent spark of disaffection was fanned into flame,' which culminated on the night of the 18th February in the wholesale plundering of Portuguese shops, not only in Georgetown, but also on the East and West Coasts, and on the banks of the Demerara River. The Government evidently took warning before the sparks developed into the final flame, for we find that upon this same date, the 18th, the Court of Policy met and passed an Ordinance to make provision 'for more effectually repressing disturbances and attempts to commit breaches of the peace.' The Ordinance was very stringent, and provided that 'any person who shall assault another not of the same race as himself, destroy property, throw stones or other missiles, or who shall carry arms or weapons in the streets, or make use of language calculated to provoke a breach of the peace, shall be liable on conviction to a fine of $100, or for imprisonment for any period of time not exceeding six months, or to be punished by flogging not exceeding 39 lashes.'

Other clauses made it illegal for more than five persons to assemble in a disorderly manner, and gave summary powers of arrest to policemen and special constables, of whom a large number were sworn in – On the night of the 18th, Charlestown was the scene of a terrible riot, and the military were called out to assist the civil authorities. Magistrates were sitting and trying offenders during the greater part of the night, when 150 people were arrested in Charlestown alone. But beyond the many cases dealt with summarily, no less than 107 rioters were sent for trial, and several were sentenced to three years' hard labour, while others were ordered to be 'catted' in the City Gaol. The destruction of property was enormous and several houses were completely demolished. The riot extended to the country districts with almost equally disastrous results, and a detachment of military was sent to Plantation Great Diamond, where the disturbances assumed a very serious characters. One of the instances of the riots was that the Chief Justice was stopped on his way to the Courts and harangued by a man named King on behalf of a tumultuous crowd of people. It was charged that the Governor was the Governor of the Portuguese and kept the black people down, and the Chief Justice while warmly repudiating the assertion admitted that the belief was common among lower classes. After agitating the whole colony for two or three days, the riots were effectually quelled, and subsequently the Portuguese shop keepers received compensation for the losses they had suffered. Considering the provocation which was offered to the Portuguese that they appeared to have done nothing except to protect their property from most unwarrantable attacks, it certainly does not seem right that the memory of these wrongs should be perpetuated by the commonly accepted phrase of the Portuguese riots. It was the superstitions and ignorant black people who did the rioting and it was the Portuguese who suffered the injury. 'Teneriffe' therefore enters a very pertinent and prosper protest against perpetual insult being added to palpable injury.

(*The Daily Chronicle*, 18 February 1887)

Our Spirit Shops

There is a general saying that 'Bread is the staff of life' but it has come to be regarded in this colony that 'Rum itself is life.' Not only is this so with those who sell and those who buy it but Government, regards this means

of taxation of the principal source of its existence, and year by year they lay increased burdens on the rum shop keepers while at the same time they increase the taxation in all possible and questionable ways. At the present day the retail tarriff of the colony is almost entirely in the hands of the Portuguese and whatever might be attempted to be said as to the sale and preparation of spirits that the Governments supervise and countenance, it cannot be denied that their palaces in the way of rum shops taverns and restaurants are as beautiful to the eye and pleasing to the customers as the fairy palaces of the gods. The rum shops is to the poor man what the clubhouse is to the rich, each feeling that there is a pleasant moment in store for him at some other place than his own home and it is only when either party takes too much that much wrong is done. The Portuguese are only properly regarded as carrying on the spirit trade of the colony and that they acquit themselves in a manner that is worthy of praise can only be instanced in the custom that they draw from all sources, the revenue that was obtained from rum last year is the largest on record and amounted to as much as $648,671,51 while the general licences only reached $78,881,68 and with the whole revenue of the year amounting to $2,082,008. It will be seen that the Portuguese spirit dealer as a collection of revenue for the colony paid in more than ¼ of the entire revenue. All of this money was gathered by 227 rum shops keepers and it is a surprise to strangers and a wonder to the islands around us that the amount of obstacles placed in the way of rum shop keepers.

They are not only able to live but by the main support of the state. A few of the regulations are so rigid that they seem to be extremely stupid. For instance a retail spirit dealer is not allowed to sell one person more than one large bottle of rum at a time (quart) without a permit but several persons can be allowed to take a quart away from the shop and for the same person. What is equally stupid is the fining of a person if he is found carrying more than a quart of rum while he might carry cases of mixed liquors without fear of fine.

Now it has been admitted by the best authorites that a good quality of rum is superior in itself to whisky and even Mr Darnell the comptroller of customs writing about it some time ago gave it the chief place of all potation. The Sunday Trading Ordinance is only known where the Portuguese spirit and provision shops exist. Some time ago a pack of vagabonds who were engaged to tempt the Portuguese spirit dealer to accommodate their masters were suddenly checked by being punished for the means they used to cause the shopkeeper to commit an offence, but it seems that this has spent itself and the bare opening of a shop for ventilation is tried to the made an offence. It is not only unfair but decidedly one sided to allow a rum shop of certain class in which must be included the clubs that are without licences and the hotels and taverns to sell all sorts of liquor on Sundays and to prevent the rum shops that pay a licence of $7,000 a year to be opened for the shortest possible time. Now we do not say that the rum shops should be opened to sell liquors on Sundays, nor are they, but surely if there is any offence at all it must be with those places who sell liquor on Sunday mornings and evenings and Magistrates Officials and Public Servants can go in and out to buy their whisky, brandy, gin and even rum, while the poor man cannot get his glass of grog which perhaps he was not able to get Saturday night, not having got his pay early enough and it is committed an offence to admit through a side door one such man at a time while another is allowed to sell with doors wide open.

Either all rumshops drinking houses and clubs should be opened all day Sunday or all closed. What can be said about spirit shops discrimination by the Portuguese when the public market is thrown open wide to the surprise of strangers and those people who could buy their meats and other articles on Saturday are accommodated with them on Sunday, yet it is wrong for the rum shop keeper to do the very thing the government is doing week after week. Let the market also be closed and if they will keep it open stop prosecutions against rum shops for selling on Sundays.

There is another hardship that is placed upon the Portuguese rum shop keepers. It is expected that the place is to be purer than any respectable hotel in the colony and the language far above that of the market place. It is required that people of ill repute do not enter their shops where as in Water Street the present day there are known common houses above stairs and no one thinks of prosecuting the merchant.

If you want to be alarmed, visit the Stabroek Market and there you will hear such a noise it will drive you mad, yet if there is a little argument or loud talking by a sailor who might have been drunk before he reached that rum shop, this is a cause for prosecution. We condemn gambling by the rich as well as by the poor, but while the government allows members of the greatest clubs in the city to game in open day, they prosecute the gambling by the Chinese in lower Charlestown. Is there not a law for all classes of the colony alike!

(*A União Portugueza* Sabado 21 Junho 1890)

Portuguese support local industry

Messrs Silva Bros forward us for inspection specimens of plantain flour, cassava flour, and Indian corm meal manufactured at their Pomeroon Factory. From what we hear of the production of these articles of consumption is likely to develop into an extensive industry in the near future. The firm we have referred to, have Thirty-Three acres under corn and cassava at Pln *Promise,* in the Pomeroon district, and they also buy largely from the people round about. The firm have imported improved machinery, including an American flour mill of the newest pattern, that will enable them to turn out from thirty to forty barrels of flour per day, and if it is all of the same excellent quality as the sample that have been forwarded to us it is difficult to imagine that it will find otherwise than a ready sale in the Colonial market. The Town agents of the firm are Messrs A C Faria Croal Street.

(Illustrates the enterprising nature of the Portuguese – dispels view that Portuguese were owners of only rum shops and provision stores).

(*The Daily Chronicle* Wed, 6 Dec 1893)

THE PREMIER MINERS' HARDWARE WAREHOUSE
Lot 23 Newtown

Wright and Butler's Kerosene Store.

Lamps, gold scales, dinner, breakfast ware, Tea Sets, Cutlery, skillets, coffee pots, frying pans stew pots, bath tubs, Sad iron, Dinner Bells, Breakfast Call Bell, Cutlasses, Kitchen Knives.

Soaps.

Overcoats, legging, cotton hammocks, etc. for Gold Diggers

Musical Boxes, Watches, Clocks

Tools of all Classes, brass foundry, all kinds of explosives, Bent wood Chairs, Rockers, for livery Stables various equipments.

Abel Maria da Silva
(Proprietor)

(*The Daily Liberal* 30 July, 1893)

Commission Agents

Theo A D'Mattos – General Commission Agent and Broker – will undertake Stock-Taking, Book-keeping, etc.

Lot 9, America Street.

(*The Daily Liberal* 1 August 1893)

LUSITANIA ICE CO LTD

Capital $50,000 divided into 1,000 shares of $50 each
First vessel arrived – Ice Establishment to be opened on Thursday, 26th
April –

one cent per pound for natural ice
19 Depots opened in Georgetown to sell their ice
5 in the country – Plaisance, Belfield, Buxton, Friendship, Bartica

Fresh fish will always be on sale. No credit but to approved
customers.
We desire to impress on the public mind that:

1st– We have no chimney on our Premises and no connection
whatever with any Ice Factory and therefore we can sell no artificial Ice.

2nd– Our Ice (as will be seen) is remarkably solid and pure and far
superior in its keeping quality to any Manufactured Ice.
The Co. would provide, besides regular supply of their favourite
Natural Ice, Fruits and other Delicacies of a northern clime, at reasonable proces, and we launch it out in the full expectation that public
support will not be withheld from it.

Manuel L. R. Andrade
Manager & Secretary

Water St., Lot 14
23rd March 1896

(The Echo, 4 April 1896)

HOTEL GRAND CENTRAL.

E'STE HOTE, pelo seu nome indica que a localidade é central. E'situado na proximidade do caes dos vapores costeiros, e do caes onde desenbarcam estrangeiros. E'o Hotel mais fresco nesta cidade, e o mais proximo para aquelles que desenbarcam de qualquer parte, onde se poderão refrescar depois da desconsolação duma longa viagem.

A BARRA

Acha-se replecta das melhores bebidas, licóres, limonadas charutos etc.,

A COSINHA

Está á testa duma bôa cosinheira e obtem-se ás horas marcadas, almoços, lunchs, jantares e seias.

QUARTOS DE DORMIR

São os mais frescos e confortaveis que se encontram nesta cidade, tendo um espaçoso e magnifico quarto de banho à disposição dos hospedes.

O SALÃO DO BILHAR

É fresquissimo, e os marcadores são delicados e attenciosos.

CREADOS

São estes os mais cortêzes e attenciosos para com todos os visitantes.

Dà-se comida mensalmente, mediante ajuste especial.

GEORGETOWN, 6, de Novembro 1897.

HOTEL GRAND CENTRAL

THIS HOTEL, as its name indicates, is in a central locality. It is situated near the steamship docks and the docks where the foreigners disembark. The hotel is the coolest in this city and the nearest for those who disembark in whatever part, when they wish to refresh themselves after the weariness of a long voyage.

BAR
Stocked with the best drinks, liqueurs, lemonades, cigars, etc.

KITCHEN
At the head of the kitchen is a good cook, and at fixed times one can obtain breakfasts, snacks, dinners and suppers.

BEDROOMS
They are the coolest and most comfortable that can be found in this city, having a spacious and magnificent bathroom at the disposal of the guests.

BILLIARD ROOM
Exceedingly cool and with polite and attentive waiters.

SERVANTS
These are the most courteous and attentive to all visitors.

Special Terms given for monthly meals
Georgetown, 6 November 1897

(*Chronica Semanal*, 13 November 1897)

ESTREBARIAS

DE

GEORGETOWN E VICTORIA

GEORGETOWN DEMERARA

Trens de todas as qualidades por preços rasoaveis.

ATTENÇÃO ESPECIAL NO ALOJAMENTO DE CAVALLOS.

FORNECEMOS CAVALLOS E CARRUAGENS

Para Casamentos, Baptisados, Visitas, e Passeios, com punctualidade.

FUNERAES

Temos sempre prompto um fornecimento de Caixões, Mortalhas, e todos os demais necessarios para

FUNERAES

As requisições desta localidade ou do campo são **satisfeitas com** promptidão a qualquer **hora do dia ou de noite.**

SOLICITAMOS PROTECÇÃO

TERMOS CONVENIENTES.

Todas as Ordens serão Attendidas

por

JOSE DE FREITAS POMBO.

Director.

Telephone   Telephone

Estrebaria Georgetown,   Estrebaria Victoria,
No. 287.   No. 94.

Georgetown, 1 Outubro 1897.

STABLES

of

GEORGETOWN AND VICTORIA

Georgetown Demerara

Troops of horses of all types at reasonable prices
Special attention given to accommodation of horses
We supply horses and carriages
For Weddings, Baptisms, Visits and Outings with punctuality
FUNERALS
We have always ready a supply of Coffins, Biers and
everything else necessary for
FUNERALS
Requests in this locality or from outside are attended to
promptly and satisfactorily at any time of day or night
We solicit patronage
Convenient terms
All orders will be attended to

by
JOSÉ DE FREITAS POMBO
Director
Stable Victoria
No. 91

Telephone
Stable Georgetown
No. 287
Georgetown, 1 October 1897

(*Chronica Semanal,* 13 November 1897)

The Kingston Cocoa and Chocolate Factory

Proprietors: D'Aguiar Bros.

We beg to thank our customers and the public generally for their patronage and increasing appreciation of our *CHOCOLATE* and *COCOA* ESSENCE and in spite of reports that may draw invidious distraction against our manufacture, we give below a statement made by one of the greatest authorities who holds the highest distinction a man of science can attain, i.e., Fellow of the Royal Society of London, writes that "Mixture of ground cocoa with starch, etc. are called Soluble Cocoa and chocolate is cocoa ground up with sugar and flavoured with vanilla, sometimes with bitter almonds as well, or with cinnamon and other spices; it generally contains some starch or flour. For general use, cocoa is a milder, less stimulating, and more nutritious beverage than tea or coffee. Next to oil and fat starch is the most concentrated, heat-giving and force producing of all the nutrients" . . .

The fact of a manufacturer submitting samples of his stuff for analysis is no guarantee that the proportions of the ingredients and the same composition will be always maintained. There is no better guarantee of the quality of an article than the inquiry in a Public Court where it has been shown to be pure, wholesome and nutritious, containing in fact over 60% of high class cocoa. We rejoice over this success as it is an advantage gained for ourselves and its consumers will be more then ever satisfied that all along they obtained the most pure, the most healthful, the most delicious, the most digestable, the most nutritious of chocolate.

We all know that Christopher Columbus and Cortes were the first to introduce chocolate in Europe, but it is news to us to be told that it was first introduced in this Colony by a man still living.

Our cocoa essence and chocolate prepared with the utmost care recommends itself by its nutritive and digestive properties as well as by its fine flavour and aroma. The constant increase in the amount of our sales demonstrates how great the appreciation it enjoys with the public, and with its increasing favour. There has been a corresponding increase of imitations. The PLANT and MACHINERY have recently been considerably increased, and enable our firm to supply a chocolate of such excellent quality at low price.

We have very recently received a few unsolicited testimonies from local gentlemen who unanimously pronounce our preparations as *excellent.*

Georgetown 28 June 1898   D'AGUIAR BROS.

(*The Daily Chronicle* 2 July, 1898)

J. A. GOMES

of the

CITY OF BARTICA

wishes to inform the public and his numerous customers and friends that, on Thursday 6th of this month, he opened a supply store at Lot 9 America Street, Georgetown with the name

BART!CA MINING SUPPLY STORE

This store will mainly serve the purpose of filling orders for foodstuffs for gold expeditions and sending them through his place in Bartica directly to Cuyuni and Puruni, at moderate and reasonable prices.

From the 16th of this month onwards, he proposes to despatch a boat every Wednesday to Bartica, Quartzstone, Cuyuni, departing at midday, and another boat on Fridays from Bartica to Bernard Landing, taking passengers, foodstuffs, etc.

Bartica Mining Store
Telephone No. 236

(*Chronica Semanal,* 15 July 1899)

The Uitlanders of B. G.
Excise and Rum duties

" . . . Where in the name of common honesty and fairplay, where in the wide world, even in the much abused and derided Transvaal, is such a system of extortion to be found? Do the public perceive how this system works, and how it does so always to the prejudice of the dealer, who is treated in this manner merely because he is a foreigner and not an Englishman? Do they now see the evident desire of the Government and governing classes to squeeze, filch and rob a hard working class of men not only of the legitimate profits of their trade, but also of the means they may have acquired by the exercise of the greatest industry, frugality and self-denial!

A storm of indignation rises in our heart, our whole soul is filled with feeling of uncontrollable, bitter resentment, when we pause to consider the treatment our countrymen receive at the hands of this colonial Government. Our pen refuses to proceed; we have not words at our command to denounce this system of taxation in fitting terms; the power of speech is inadequate to paint such gross injustice and oppression in its true colours. Recalling to memory the terms used by the Rev. Parker some months back when referring to the Sultan and his Government, we can only say: *God damn the laws of the British Guiana that upholds such gross injustice.* May God's curse rest on a Government and men who derise such laws. May the ruin, misery and distress they in their injustice and malice bring down on others follows them in all their ventures.

☆　☆　☆　☆　☆　☆　☆　☆　☆

Let us now compare the system of taxation in force for the retail spirit trade, with the system of taxation that governs the trade of those sections of the community other than the *Uitlanders.* We will take, for example, a similar article of trade 'spirituous liquors'. It is chiefly in the hands of the English importer. He is not *assesses to sell* any given quantity, but has to pay a licence duty of $100 per annum, which enables him to sell any quantity, even to a million gallons if he finds the sale for them; the customs duty being $3:20 per gallon of any strength which he pays only on the actual quantity imported.

Thus Rum the poor mans' drink has to pay the pipes, being made to contribute duty on the proof gallon. Moreover, when once he has paid duty on his importations, he is not called upon to pay duty again on any stock thereof he may have in hand at the commencement of the next financial year, even though such stock may consist of thousands of gallons of whisky, gin, brandy, wines and malt liquors. So much for the spirit of justice that guides the actions of the colonial government. It is based on that principle that caused the War Office in 1809 to instruct Wellington in the Peninsula *to spare the British troops.* The policy here seems to be spare the English section of the community, be the cost whatever it may to the rest of the inhabitants of this colony.

The population of British Guiana is roughly speaking about 300,000. The Portuguese community, as a whole, number about 17,000, or 5.66% of the entire population.

The revnue of the colony in 1897-1898 was $2,425:769,34, yet if we take into account all sources of revenue, we find the Portuguese paying more than ⅓ of the revenue collected!!! It may be urged as it was urged by an Englishman many years ago, that if they are dissatisfied with the fiscal laws here, why do they not close up and leave the colony? That is also what the Boers said to the English. The question is a very plausible one, and I know that many of my countrymen would gladly do so, were it not that they would have to abandon the remnants of what cost them so much toil and privation to accumulate. Is that another desire of the colonial Government?

But unfortunately for these people such a step cannot be taken without being attended with exceedingly heavy loss to them.

We have spoken above of the bond each dealer is compelled to give. Besides that he is in nine cases out of ten the owner of the property in which he carried on his business.

Should he close, the property, for which probably he may have paid a very large sum would not find a purchaser, in the present state of the colony, perhaps not even for ¼ of the sum given for it.

Very probably also he may have paid a very high price for the good will of his business under the persuasion that the Government would not only treat him equitably, but would do all in its power to ameliorate his position as a tax payer. He confided in Colonial English justice and fairplay!

The Government is aware of all these facts and uses them to oppress the *Uitlander* and screw as much out of him as it possibly can in order to keep up a bloated civil administration that is the real cause of the ruin and distress that is spreading over the land. And the Portuguese who are famous for their patient and hard-working disposition have borne with all kinds of hard-ships and disadvantages, until these have become so oppressive and unbearable that it is a marvel to us how any human beings could have put up with the burden for such a length of time.

Even the Balaams' ass protested against the cruelty of his rider.

And as regards the moval aspect of the question, what shall we say? The Government and governing classes are always telling us in the most unctuous terms of their deep anxiety for the uplifting and betterment of the masses, yet how their actions belie their words! it is the old, old story of the bible in one hand and the rum bottle in the other.

But this article has gone beyond its accorded space and we must fain bring it to a close.

In our next we shall deal with the other store and shop licences and the Vlissengen Special Rate in their bearing towards the *Uitlander* community.

M. L. R. ANDRADE

(Chronica Semanal 11 November, 1899)

Portuguese Businessmen

Shipping Agent – Mr. John Fernandes. "A shipping agent of George-town has placed part of his office at the service of the Apostleship of the Sea. The Apostulatus Maris. Service sign affixed to the building directs the sailors to the room where they can foregather, write their letters, and read the Catholic newspapers . . . "

(Missionary Magazine, Vol. 2, No. 9. January. 1937, p.5)

Hon John Fernandes, OBE.
Merchant and Shipping Agent

D. M. Fernandes, Ltd.,

AGENTS FOR

JONES SEWING MACHINES

AND

GAZELLE CYCLES.

26, MAIN STREET,

GEORGETOWN, DEMERARA,

BRITISH GUIANA.

Cables : " DEMCYCO."

PHONE C. 483.

P.O. BOX 66.

Mr Celestine de Freitas Dies in London

The death of Mr. Celestine De Freitas prominent businessman and Governing Director of The Central Garage, occurred in a London hospital early last Friday evening on the eve of his birthday.

The sad news was cabled to his relatives in the colony by his wife, who is also in England.

Mr. De Freitas left the colony early in July of this year for medical attention in England. It is understood that he underwent an operation about two weeks ago, and showed some signs of improvement.

After leaving school Mr. de Freitas joined the Central Garage with his brother in 1927. In 1945, became the proprietor of the firm and later governing-director.

COMMUNITY SHOCKED

The news of Mr. de Freitas' passing came as a great shock to the entire community. He was a devout member of the Roman Catholic Church and held executive offices in various Councils of management, societies and associations. He was treasurer of Our Lady's Conference of St. Vincent De Paul and also served as a member of the Council of management of St. Joseph's Mercy Hospital.

In the commercial field he took a keen interest and was an executive of the Committee of the Catholic Employees' Association.

He showed keen interest in tennis and had on a few occasions represented Portuguese Club of which he was President for the past three years.

He is survived by his wife Mrs. Zelia de Freitas, two sons John and Philip and a daughter Noelle, who are at present in London.

Up to late last night no arrangements in connection with Mr. de Freitas' body being brought to the city were made available to the Press.

G Bettencourt & Company Limited

G Bettencourt & Company Limited was established in 1884 at Buxton. In 1886 the Standard opened – Wallis & Paul. 1901 Standard Dry Goods Store where Sandbach Parker Limited are today. Present Unique – Klein Limited & Drug. In 1901 Business on ground floor. 1902 Unique Retail in Bookers Sports Dept. Store. 1903 Wholesale established at top flat of Unique Store. 1906 Unique opened at present site. Standard Store closed down.

On 29th June (Circa) 1959, Messrs G Bettencourt & Company Limited celebrated their 75th Anniversary.

The Founder, the late Mr Gregorio Bettencourt born in Porto Santo, a small island near Madeira, first commenced business in Buxton in 1884 but moved to Georgetown in 1886 where he opened The Standard Retail Dry Goods Store in Water Street on part of the site presently occupied by Sandbach Parker & Company Limited.

In 1901 a Wholesale Department was also established in hired premises on the first floor of the present Bettencourts Building and a second Retail Store called The Unique was opened in part of the premises now occupied by Bookers Cycle & Sports Department.

In 1906 the present building at 19 Water Street was purchased and The Unique Retail was transfered to the Ground Floor where it had been trading for 73 years. Later the same year The Standard Dry Goods Store was closed down and both the Wholesale and Retail departments traded under the name of G Bettencourt & Company Wholesale & Retail Merchants.

On the 10th March, 1908, a public company was floated under the name of G Bettencourt & Company Limited and the entire Share Capital of $200,000.00 (since increased) was fully subscribed. The first Chairman of the newly formed Company was the late Mr J B Laing, Managing Director of the British Guiana Bank since absorbed by the Royal Bank of Canada.

Mr G Bettencourt retired on the foundation of the public company but remained as a Director till his death in 1919 at the age of 90.

Mr John Hird of Manchester a personal friend of Mr Bettencourt was the United Kingdom representative of the firm from 1906 till 1919 when Messrs James J Sabey & Sons Limited were appointed but in 1930

G Bettencourt & Company Limited was registered in the United Kingdom and an Office opened under their own name in London.

A Branch Store was established in Paramaribo in 1912 and continued till 1940 when financial control became difficult during the last war and it was sold to a resident of Surinam.

Between the years 1933 and 1953 the financial control was gradually acquired by G A Gomes Limited, a family company entirely owned by the remaining descendants of the founder and in 1954 G Bettencourt & Company Limited became a Private Company.

G Bettencourt & Company Limited was destroyed by fire on the 17th October, 1979, but continued trading from a Stock Room in America Stret behind the gutted Unique Store until the end of May 1984 when it went into Voluntary Liquidation.

Bettencourt family of G. Bettencourt & Co. related to Christopher Columbus

The family of G. Bettencourt was related to Christopher Columbus through Filipa Perestrello, wife of Christopher Columbus. She was the daughter of Bartholomew Perestrello who colonised Porto Santo, as Hereditary Captain. Filipa's mother was a direct ancestor of Egas Moniz, a famous Knight who in the 12th century helped establish Portugal as a separate Kingdom.

The name Perestrello was changed to Bettencourt in British Guiana because the British found it difficult to pronounce.

[This information was given by Clive Bettencourt Gomes whose great-grandfather was Gregorio Perestrello the descendant of Filipa Perestrello].

Mr S S De Freitas. Governing Director of The Charlestown Saw Mills. Ltd.

THE CONSULATE OF PORTUGAL IN BRITISH GUIANA.

Top : Senhor SYLVESTRE SYLVÃO de FREITAS. the Consul ad honorem for Portugal in British Guiana took office on July 19. 1928. three months after Dr. Oliveira Salazar became Minister of Finance. Senhor de Freitas succeeded Dr. Joaquim de Barros Ferreira da Silva who left the Colony in June, 1928. for the Consulate in Hong-Kong. later going to the Embassy in London. In private life. Senhor de Freitas is Governing-Director of the Charlestown Saw Mills, Ltd., George-town.

THE SUN, printed by the 'Daily Chronicle' Ltd, at Lots 23 and 24 Main Street, South Cummingsburg, Georgetown, for the Proprietor and Publisher, Peter Stanislaus D'Aguiar of Public Road, Kitty, East Coast, Demarara.

The Coelho-Menezes Provision and Spirit Shop, Parika

The Britannica Fashion Store, proprietor: J Nunes

Lopes, Fernandes & Co Ltd

Movement between British Guiana and Madeira

There was not only movement of goods between Madeira and British Guiana but Madeirans also returned home either with monies to support families left behind, or for a holiday, especially near the end of the 19th century and early 20th as seen from the passenger lists.

There was also a brisk trade in foodstuffs which formed a major part of the Madeiran cuisine and were transported to Demerara. The Madeirans loved their garlic, onions, potatoes, and saltfish as well as their famous Madeiran wines.

'Zargo' leaves Madeira for Demerara with cargo for Portuguese

26 August – Portuguese Barque – ZARGO – Demerara – 15 passengers (William Newton – 12 labourers, 1 woman and one minor), 13 pipes and 3 cases of wine, 136 casks and 1,000 arrobas* of onions and 162 casks of potatoes and various other things.

(*O Defensor,* N.192, Sabado de Septembro de 1843, vol.iv)

26 Agosto. Pat. Port. ZARGO – Demerara – 15 pass. (William Newton, 12 trabalhadores, 1 mulher e l menor) 13 pipas e 3 caixoes de vinho, 136 barris e 1,000 arrobas de sebolas, e 162 barris de batatas e varios outros generos.

*(arroba = 32 lbs in Portugal)

MADEIRA WINE

MADEIRA WINE COMPANY, LDA.

AVENIDA ARRIAGA, 28

P. O. BOX 295, FUNCHAL, ISLAND OF MADEIRA

(PORTUGAL)

6 - 84

Shipments of Wine from Alfandega do Funchal, January-June 1843

Demerara	35 pipes	St. Vincent	31 pipes
Antigua	20 pipes	St. Thomas	19 pipes
Barbados	70 pipes	Trinidad	23 pipes
Grenada	25 pipes	Nassau	15 pipes
Jamaica	278 pipes	Nevis	2 pipes
Kingston	8 pipes	St. Petersburg	2,185 pipes
St. Kitts	22 pipes	London	1,138 pipes

(*O Imparcial*, No. 163, 20 October 1843)

Shipments of Wine from Alfandega do Funchal July-December 1843

Antigua	17 pipes	Nevis	2 pipes
Barbados	76 pipes	St. Kitts	23 pipes
Bermudas	1 pipe	St. Thomas	4 pipes
Demerara	49 pipes	St. Vincent	44 pipes
Grenada	14 pipes	Trinidad	11 pipes
Jamaica	319 pipes	Tobago	9 pipes
Kingston	3 pipes	London	621 pipes

(*O Imparcial*, No. 182, 3 March 1844)

PARA DEMARARA
REGISTER OF PASSPORTS: Funchal, Madeira

No. 51   Antonio Lopes Sardinha – 27 years – small eyes, natural complexion, etc. his wife, Josepha Pereira Garcez, 24 years and their servant, Francisco, 19 years, exempt from basic military training because of rupture.

Calheta – 27 August 1853

No. 52   Isilino Roiz da Camara – 28 years, medium height, small eyes, natural complexion – his wife, Maria de Souza Caldeira – 26 years and children, João, 5 years, Christina 4 and Juliana, a nursing child, their pupil, Silvester, 14 years.

Calheta, 27 August 1853

No. 56   José Ferreira – 40 years, 62 ins, swarthy complexion . . . his wife Antonia de M^{ca} – 30 years and children, Manoel 2 years and Maria 5 years.

Machico – 27 August 1853

No. 57   João José de Mendonca Furtado – 33 years, 61 ins, natural complexion his wife Theresa de Jesus, 32 years and sons, Antonio – 8 years, Manoel – 4, Joao – 2 and their servant girl, Francisca de Jesus, 26 years.

Machico – 27 August 1853

(*Registo de passaportes.* No. 749 – Governo Civil do Funchal)

'A Razao' Saturday 21st August 1867

TO DEMARARA:

The Portugueses brig Freitas brothers will leave without fail for the above mentioned port on 8th September next. The ship according to information recently received from Port Meadway U.S. ought to arrive soon.

This ship is of 235 tons and has been classified as first class, having good accomodation for passengers both in cabins and in the hold.

The price for passengers is 40,000 reis in a cabin and 25,000 reis in the hold. Good treatment is guaranteed.

Also freight will be carried for a very reasonable price.

All those interested in freight or passages ought to contact the office of the late Joao de Freitas Martins, in the Tanoeiros Road.

Funchal 14th August 1867

TO DEMERARA:

On the 5th of September next there ought to leave without fail the portuguese Patacho pinnace 'Greyhound' with Captain Avellar. It has the best accomodation for passangers.

For cargo and passages please deal with the office of A.F. Camacho and Sons. Constitution Square, Funchal 14th August 1869.

'AS NOVIDADES'

Thursday 21st February 1867

TO DEMERARA:

The Portugues brig Freitas brothers captained by Manuel Rodrigues Conde is expected to arrive soon from Lisbon according to news received from the steampship 'Lusitania'. It will leave for the above mentioned port between now and the 5th of March, next without fail.

This pleasant ship has magnificent accomodation for passengers, it is swift and because of recent repairs it has been reclassified as first class for the next two years.

For the reception of passengers in cabins and the prow as well as cargo please contact the office of Joao de Freitas Martins in the Rua de Tanoeiros.

Movement of Ships from Madeira to Demerara
Embarcaçoes/Sahidas

Escuna port. *Graciosa,* para Demerara, 3 passeigeiros, Alipio A. Ferreira e outros, carga – cebola e diversos generos.

(*A Razão,* Sabbado, 2 de julho, 1871)

Hiate port. *Aveirense,* para Demerara, 74 passageiros (colonos), carga – diversos generos.

(*A Razão,* Sabbado, 12 de Octubro, 1872)

Escuna port. *Cidade de Belem,* para Demerara, 53 passageiros (colonos), carga – diversos generos.

(*A Razão,* Sabbado, 26 de Octubro, 1872)

Patacho port. *Camaco* 1, para Demerara, 14 passageiros (colonos) – carga – semilha e cebola.

(*A Razão,* Sabbado, 12 de julho, 1873)

Barca ing. *E.W. Cohoon,* para Demerara, 146 passageiros (colonos), carga – diversos generos.

(*A Razão,* Sabbado, 13 de Setembro, 1873)

Hiate port. *Tres Irmaos,* para Demerara e Berbice, carga – diversos generos.

(*A Razão,* Sabbado, 25 de Octubro, 1873)

Patacho port. *Novo Mathilde,* para Demerara, 49 passageiros (colos); carga – varios generos.

(*A Razão,* Sabbado, 1 de Novembro, 1873)

Passengers for Madeira

Per brigt. *Camacho* 1°, on the 5th instant: For Madeira. – José Gonsalves, Ludovina Gonsalves, Antonio, Francisco, José, and Maria, filhos, Luzia De Freitas, Christina, filha, Manoel Martins Ribeiro, Leonilda, filha, Edwardo and João, filhos, Joaquim Gonsalves, Manoel Mendonca, Jr., D'Umbelina A. Mendonca, D. Leonilda, and D. Maria, filhas Gerarda, Creada, Manoel Fernandes Paulino, Francisco Moniz, Francisca, filha, Manoel Antonio de Silva, José de Castro, Carolina Augusta Gonsalves, João Ferreira de Menzies, Manoel Fernandes dos Santos, Julio dos Santos Olimo, Domengos da Silva Maio, Manoel Correa, Antonio de Souza, João Souza, filho, Maria C.M. da Paixao, Maria M. d'Assumpeao, Henrique Assumparo Alexandrina de Souza, Albino, filho, Luzia, filho, Maria Lucia de Jesus Jacinto de Freitas, João, filho, Maria, Alexandrina, Maria, filhas, Anna Roiz Teixera, Damiao Lopez, Cardoza, Roza de Souza, Francisco de Franca, Maria Freire França, Joauna, filha Joaquina C. Viera, Augusto Mendonca, Rosa Matilde Pestano, Antonio Fernandes Serralha, Joaquina Gomes, Maria, filha, Manoel Rodrigues, Sr., Palmira A. de Jesus, Anna Roiz Teixeira, Maria, filha, Maria Moniz, José Fernandes, Jesuina de Pontes, Maria Gonsalves, Manoel Da Silva, Joanna de Silva, João, filho, Maria Carolina de Freitas, Maria Conceicao Jesus, José, filho Natividade, Ermilinda, filias, Antonio Camara, and Beatrice de Souza.

(*The Daily Chronicle* Thurs. 6 July 1882)

Passengers from Madeira

(Passenger List)

1st Class – Mr. Manl Gomes, Mrs. Gomes, Miss R. Gomes, Miss Govia, Mrs J.A. Ferreira, Mr. G. J. Fernandez, Mr. J. A. Perreira, Mr. M. S. Ferreira, Mrs. Ferreira, Miss Coelho, Mr. Antonio Ferreira, Mrs. Antonio Ferreira and Mr. José Gomes. 2nd Class – Mr. F. dos Reis, Mr. Alex. D'Ornellas, Mr. R. T. Macedo, Mr. Antonio De Souza, Mrs. De Souza, Miss De Souza, and servant, Mrs. C. D'Andrade, Miss D'Andrade Mr. G. F. Da Costa, Mrs. Da Costa, Mr. Da Costa, jnr., Mr. Antonio Ferreira, Mrs. Ferreira, Mrs. F. F. Dos Santos, Mr. J. C. Vieira, Mrs. Vieira and child, Mr. J. G. Ramalho, Mr. J. R. Gouvia, Mrs. Gouvia, Miss Gouvia, Miss Gomes, Mr. A. R. de Freitas, Mr. José Gomes, Mr. F. B. Cunha, Mr. M. G. Rodrigues, Mrs. Rodrigues, 3 children and servant, Mr. Maul. Francino, Mr. M. de F. Carrega, and 3 children, Mr. J. D'Andrade, Mr. Antonio Correa, Mr. J. Gomes, Miss Gomes, Mr. M. Fernandes and Mr. J. M. Gomes.

(*The Daily Chronicle* Fri. 22 Sept. 1893)

Passengers from Madeira

53 Passengers on the S. S. *Nonpareil* – including children and maids Return to Madeira – 13 Jan – 14 passengers among them Mr. and Mrs. Gomes, 3 children and *nurse* (1st Class)
Fares by *Nonpareil* – La Penitence Wharf
To Madeira 1st Class – $75.00
To Madeira 2nd Class – $50.00
To London – £17.10

(*Dem. Daily Chronicle* Mail Edn. 8 Jan 1887)

Trade with Madeira
SHIPPING NEWS
Entered – July 6th

FELISBERTA, A Barque 25 days from Madeira, Rolla, 297 tons, 13 men to Rodrigues and Abreu – 2,020 hampers, 602 boxes and 2 brls potatoes, 5 cases and 1 demijohn wine, 50 cases garlic, 3 brls albacore (fish), 216,600 lbs. onions and 345 bags coriander seeds also cargo for other ports for re-exportation.

(*The Daily Chronical,* Wednesday, 6 July 1898)

Madeira Banana brought from Demerara

"Banana – The most common type today is a variety of the *Musa Cavendishi . . . ,* better known in Madeira as the dwarf banana, which was introduced in 1842, having its origin in China but transplanted in this archipelago by means of samples brought from Demerara, by reason of which it is also called the *Demerara banana."*

(Translated from Eduardo C.N. Pereira. *Ilhas de Zargo.* Vol. 1, 2 Edição Câmara Municipal do Funchal, 1956)

The Portuguese and The Church

It is mainly due to the Portuguese with their long tradition of Catholicism that the Catholic Church in British Guiana was firmly established and expanded through the years. The Portuguese government was concerned that their countrymen would receive the services of a priest and petitioned the British government accordingly. Although the Colonial Secretary agreed with this request the Combined Court in British Guiana objected as it meant financial support. In 1845 the Catholic Committee petitioned the Court of Policy reminding the members that they also contributed to the "public burdens of taxation".

A memorable event for the Portuguese was the arrival of a Portuguese priest in 1845. During the following years it was difficult if not impossible to procure Portuguese priests so Italian priests who spoke Portuguese were introduced, among them memorable figures such as Fathers Gambetti, Schembri, Mesini, Negri, Casati, and many others.

The Madeiran Portuguese, as they were used to do in their island home, celebrated their special feast days with all the pomp, pageantry and piety which were part and parcel of their religious lives. These celebrations of the main Portuguese feasts – The Feast of Pentecost, St. Anthony, St. Philomena, St. John the Baptist, St. Peter, and, above all, Nossa Senhora do Monte (Our Lady of the Mount – patron of Madeira) were explosions of faith highlighted by Solemn High Mass, Vespers, processions and Benediction of the Blessed Sacrament. Special trains offering excursion fares were put on to transport the Portuguese faithful to feasts held in Plaisance, Buxton, Victoria and Belfield. The accounts of these feasts as will be noted describe the elaborate decorations in the church, the flowers, the arches, the bunting, the flags and the lights. Fireworks were a *sine qua non* of all the main festivals. The Jubilee of Pope Leo XIII lavishly celebrated in 1893 at Sacred Heart Church seemed to reach the apogee in Portuguese religious celebrations. The local press spoke in glowing terms of the festivities remarking that "in the evening one of the grandest illuminations ever witnessed in the city was displayed in front of the Church of the Sacred Heart." The electric lights numbered 300, the Chinese lanterns 400, and the fairy lamps over 2,000! Crowds of Guyanese gathered to witness the proceedings further enlivened by the famous Portuguese band of the First of December.

It was indeed fitting to have such celebrations at Sacred Heart Church which had been built and financed by the Portuguese in 1861 and today now ranks as our National Shrine. During the 1940s to the 1960s Sacred Heart Church was very much noted for the solemn and colourful May processions in honour of Our Lady of Fatima. The excerpt on the celebration of the Feast of St. Philomena reminds one of the great devotion which the young Portuguese girls had for this saint.

But the main religious celebration introduced by the Madeiran Portuguese was the Christmas Novena which still remains an integral part of the preparations for Christmas. In the early hours of the morning or in the evening (a recent innovation) the Novena is attended not only by Portuguese but by Guyanese of all ethnic groups and from every walk of life. From 16th to 23rd December the BEMDITA, the Portuguese hymn sung before the Novena Mass still re-echoes throughout Guyana.

Priest Services for Portuguese

Downing Street
27th December, 1841

Sir,
I have received your Despatch, No. 129, of the 13th October, on the state of the Portuguese immigrants, and your Despatch, No. 140, of the 24th October, further on the same subject, and on the subject of the immigrants generally.

The accounts given in these Despatches, and their enclosures, show that it will be necessary to watch very carefully the further progress of the Portuguese immigration, and I beg to express to you the satisfaction which it has been me to observe the great care and attention which you have paid to the subject, as well as the grounds you have stated for being yourself satisfied with the care taken of the immigrants by their employers.

I have thought it right to communicate copies of your Despatches to the Portuguese Minister at this Court, and to Promise to communicate the further reports which you will no doubt furnish me from time to time.

I have also stated, with reference to the great distress which is suffered by the immigrants through deprivation of religious offices and consolations, that if the Portuguese Government should be desirous to send a priest of that nation to British Guiana, I trust that you would be enable, by the assistance of the Combined Court, to provide for his reception and accommodation, and I beg to recommend the subject to your consideration; and I should be glad to learn that after consultation with the Combined Court, you would enable me to make a definite proposal to the Portuguese Government.

You will, no doubt, continue to pay the most careful attention to the question of the medical attendance furnished to the immigrants, and in addition to any measures which you may adopt for increasing the number of public hospitals and dispensaries, I think it very desirable that, as far as you can, without giving rise to any complaint of official interference with private arrangements, you should bring the subject under the consideration of individual planters, letting it be understood that any advice which may be given by the authorities as to the distribution of immigrants, will be especially guided by the sufficiency of the provision for the sick, made upon the plantation at the expense of the proprietor.

In the report of the Commissioners of Inquiry of the 15th September, and in Mr. Humphrey's letter of the 24th September, it is stated that the Portuguese on "Plantation Lima" attributed the mortality on that estate in some measure to the immigrants having been kept under closed hatches whilst on their voyage, owing to a suspicion of mutiny entertained by the captain. It would be desirable to make inquiry into the circumstances of the case, in order to ascertain whether the conduct of the captain was justifiable.

(Lord Stanley to Governor Light, No. 47, 27 December 1841)

C. C. Not Amenable to R. C. Priest for Portuguese

I regret, for the sake of the colony, that the climate is so unfavourable to the Portuguese, though the temperature is not, perhaps, higher than in their native island. In health, they are a most industrious, hard working, and hitherto most honest and submissive race.

Those who remain in town, as shopkeepers and hucksters, though often sickly, are useful, they accumulate money by small gains and great economy, and many of them will acquire comparative wealth, which of course will not remain in this colony.

Your Lordship will have seen in the estimate for the year 1842, that a blank had been left there, on the application of Bishop Clancy, for four additional Roman Catholic priests; but from the temper of the non-official section of the Court of Policy, I do not expect that any sum will be voted in Combined Court. This is not just, and would have been good reason for the Portuguese Government apposing emigration from Madeira had it been advisable to continue it.

An allusion to the treatment of the Portuguese on their passage from Madeira, in the schooner Rienzi, as probably affecting their health, I refer your Lordship to my Despatch, No. 83, date 6th July, where I stated the circumstances connected with the fact. The captain, a subject of the United States, was fined 100 dollars and imprisoned 14 days, this, with the law expenses and the loss of 40 dollars a-day demurrage would probably be a lesson to him for an imprudence resulting from the unnecessary fears which, happily for him, as well as for the emigrants, were not attended during the voyage with any fatal results, however much those fears may have led to unfavourable termination of disease after the emigrants landed.

(Governor Henry Light to Lord Stanley, No. 73, 24th January 1842.)

To His Excellency Hon. Light Esq.,
Governor and Commander in Chief

The Honourable The Court of Policy,
and the Financial Representatives in Combined Court assembled.

The Humble petition of the undersigned, Roman Catholic inhabitants of this colony, for themselves and on behalf of their fellow subjects and colonists of the same faith

Respectfully sheweth –
that your petitioners have learnt with great regret, that an application of their Bishop the Right Hon, Dr. Hynes to your Hon. Court for an increased grant of money for Catholic Purposes has been refused.

Your petitioners beg most respectfully to state that the Catholic inhabitants amount fully to one tenth of the entire population of the Province, and that they contribute a full quota to the public burdens of taxation.

Your petitioners respectfully claim for themselves and their co-religionists equal rights, and priveleges, and an equal share in the benefits arising from the expenditure of the Public monies, as is enjoyed by the members of the Anglican and Presbyterian Churches. That when the Legislature of this province was anxious to procure labourers by Emigration from Madeira, the Hon. the Court of Policy gave a distinct and positive pledge that if Catholic Immigrants arrived in British Guiana they, (the Court) would provide support for additional Catholic priests the non fulfilment of which pledge will (amongst other evils) assuredly in time lead the most valuable of these people to withdraw themselves and capital from this province and check if not supress emigration from that country.

That your petitioners though fully aware of their perfect right to claim by petition to your Hon. Court pecuniary assistance for the purposes of this church have acted with greater forbearance than other religionists, having only applied for a grant of money *once in nineteen years!!!*

Your petitioners beg most respectfully to draw your attention to the great change which the increased number of Catholics in this Province rendered necessary, and has led to, in their Ecclesiastical establishment and appeal to your individual feelings of liberality and sense of evenhanded justice in favour of their claim that the same amount of Colonial allowance should be made in favour of the Head of Senior Ecclesiastical of their Church in this province, as enjoyed by the Venerable Archdeacon Lugar and the Rev. Dr. Struthers.

That your Petitioners in claiming these rights and in maintaining this equality, wish to do so in the most respectful manner, and beg to draw your honourable Court's attention to the danger to immigration in general which would most probably follow a refusal to fulfil the pledge made by your Hon. Court in reference to the Portuguese, previous to their arrival, to provide for their spiritual wants, the enemies to Immigration might then fairly argue, that *Faith Broken with Portuguese Catholics on Religious Affairs, would not be kept with Hindoos, and others* on subjects affecting their general comforts and interests a consideration we believe of great moment at this juncture.

Your petitioners regret to mention that the Catholic Church on Brid Dam is in a dilapidated state and fast hastening to decay, a condition alike distressing to your Memorialists and discrediting to this Province. That on the Arabian Coast and other districts there beside many thousand Catholics who have no opportunity of attending to their religious duties, and have no school for the education of their children, an evil great and alarming, for we beg to assure your Honbl. Court that though from these causes, these individuals may become Lax Catholics they will certainly make but indifferent members of any other Religion, and good order and Morality are sure to suffer.

Your petitioners most humbly pray therefore that your Execellency and Honbl. Court will grant unto their Bishop such increased allowance as will make his income equal to those of senior ecclesiastics before-named – that you will make provision for the support and maintenance of an increased number of priests and Cathecists, especially with the view of instructing the Portuguese – and that you will grant unto your petitioners a sum of money adequate to defraying the expense of repairing their Church in Georgetown and to provide three small, plain, unostenatious buildings as Chapels, indispensably necessary for the increased wants of the Community.

And your petitioners as in duty bound will every pray:

John McDonnell R.C. Pastor of Berbice
Jon. . . . . . . Schads   Members of the Catholic Committee.
John Taggart

Georgetown Demerary, 17th March 1845.

First Portuguese Priest

With a view of benefiting the Portuguese Catholics Bishop Haynes brought out from Lisbon in August of the year when he was enable to enter tranquilly on his episcopacy, Senor Joaquin Antonio Correa de Natividade, who was ordained a priest on *Oct. 5, 1845*. After the ceremony Father Natividade preached a sermon in Portuguese, the building being filled with immigrants of that nationality. This was the first address the people had heard in their own tongue, and it was recorded:- Like the Jews of old "who wept when the language of their native land met their ear," those hardy immigrants evinced by their sobs and tears the depth of their own patriotic feeling and the moving character of the Rev. Senor Correa's eloquence.

(The Daily Chronicle 18 June, 1893)

Ursuline Sisters come to British Guiana to teach Portuguese Children

On *29 June 1847* the Ursuline sisters came at the request of Bishop Hynes, O.P., Vicar Apostlic for British Guiana to make a foundation to provide Catholic education for the children of Portuguese immigrants.

(Ursuline Centenary Booklet, 1947)

Portuguese on Wakenham Attend Anglican Church Services

"The Portuguese also, I am happy to say, are evincing a disposition not only to send their children to our Schools [there were two – one on Pln. Zeelandia and one on Pln. Meerzorg] but to rent seats in our churches, a glaring instance of which has just occurred at Zeelandia. One Mr. Joseph Gonsalves, his wife, two daughters and Clerk, for he keeps a shop not far from the Chapel, have rented between them a pew, and are constant attenders.

Mr. G. will also no doubt willingly contribute towards our Society when officially called upon to do so."

(M.B. Johnson to Rev. E. Hawkins of SPC, Wakenham, 24 December 1855 USPG, Box 1789 – British Guiana)

Portuguese in Beterverwagting District seek services of Anglican Church

"I am pleased to be able to state that the Portuguese in this Parish have shewn some desire for religious instruction, and a service in their own language. There is no Romish priest in this district, and we are called upon to bury, baptise, and perform other rites of the Church which the Rector of St. Paul's, the Rev. F.J. Wyatt and myself are enabled to perform in their own language. We also have hopes of opening a weekly service for them in the Parish Church and are at present preparing everything for that purpose. We have five intelligent Portuguese the only ones in the village who can read, now attending our practices and trust with God's blessing on the undertaking shortly to place before these benighted people the Gospel in all its purity and simplicity."

(Charles Conyers to Secretary of SPG, 14 January 1856, USPG Box 1769, British Guiana)

[It was obvious that the Portuguese were so avid for religious instruction and services in their own language so that in places where there was no Catholic priest they attended the Anglican church.]

Registry of Wills No. 49 (Madeira)

Registered will of Maria Gonsalves Farinha – I bequeath to the Catholic Church in Main Street in the City of Georgetown, B.G. the sum of 100,000 – reis with an identical charge of 2 masses annually one for me the other for my husband on our birthdays. I leave the poor house in Demerara, B.G. a 100,000 – reis.

Sacred Heart Church 1861

(1858-1877) Bishop Ethenridge was the Bishop who saw the necessity of erecting another church in Georgetown to provide especially for the spiritual welfare of the Portuguese. On April 14, 1860 a site was bought for this purpose in Main Street for $1,870. Father James Jones, the Vicar-General negotiated the purchase, and a contract was signed for $12,000.

On Christmas Day 1861 The Church of the Sacred Heart, Main Street was opened by Father Benedict Schembri for Midnight Mass and was Solemnly blessed by Bishop Etheridge on 22 June 1861.

(*Catholic Standard* June 1961)

The Feast of the Pentecost

The Portuguese of Georgetown intend on Sunday next to celebrate the feast of Pentecost at the Royal Hotel, Main Street where the indigent will receive a substantial dinner and a supply of clothing. This is very creditable and it is not the only occasion where the wealthier classes of Portuguese have extended the hand of charity to the poor of the city. The rooms will be beautifully decorated and opened on Sunday evening for inspection. On Sunday morning a procession will form at the 'rooms' and proceed to the Roman Catholic Church where High Mass will be celebrated.

(*The Royal Gazette* Sat. May 22, 1858)

East Coast Notes

The feast of Pentecost was celebrated at the Roman Catholic Church, Victoria, with befitting solemnity and devotion. The Church was beautifully decorated by the brothers of the Society of the Sacred Heart of Jesus – the walls having been hung with rich hangings and trophies of flags. For the convenience of those desirous of attending the feast, a special train was run by the Manager of hte Demerara Railway Company leaving Georgetown at 10.30am, and stopping at all the stations, from Plaisance to Belfield via Clonbrook and back; bringing a large number of passengers chiefly Portuguese. On arrival of the train from Clonbrook, the Portuguese Band "Primeiro de Decembro" with the visitors marched to the church. Pontifical High Mass was then sung, Father Baroni being the celebrant whilst His Lordship Bishop Butler assisted (in coram) and occupied the Episcopal Chair. The Kyrie, Gloria, Credo, Sanctus, Benedictus and Agnus Dei from the music "Lugi Bordeaux" was sung by the Choir. At the "Offertory," The "O Salutaris Hostia" was effectively rendered by Mr. C. Reis. Before the Gospel of St. John the Papal Blessing was given by His Lordship. At the conclusion of Mass a eloquent Sermon was delivered on "The Holy Ghost come down on His Apostles." After that a procession was formed, headed by the cross-bearer and boys with lighted torches, followed by the several confraternities who were distinguished by their gaudy attired regalias and cappas carrying their banners. A beautiful canopy was carried over the Bishop by six of the brothers of the Sacred Heart Society, marching around the Church where there was a canvas tent erected on the processional walk a few days previous by Father Baroni. It was a great boon to the processionists. On re-entering the Sacred edifice benediction of the most blessed Sacrament was given. A few prayers were after words offered and the choir sang him:-

Holy Spirit! Lord of Light!
From Thy clear celestial height
Thy pure beaming radiance give;
Come, though Father of the poor!
Come, with treasures which endure!
Come thou Light of all that live.

After which the procession was again formed with 12 paupers in attendance, and marched to the school which was beautifully decorated with flags and coconut branches and where a hearty dinner was served to the paupers. After enjoying the delicacies they were given each a suit of clothes, a few shillings, a plate, bread, and a towel in remembrance of the occasion. The Portuguese Band discoursed sacred pieces during the day and at 5 o'clock p.m., all wended their way to the station preparatory to returning to their destination. Both the ordinary and special Trains were literally packed when leaving Belfield Station. The behaviour of the people throughout the day was anything orderly.

NOTICE
(Re Feast of the Holy Spirit)

Mr João Gonsalves, resident of Malgre Tout, emperor of the dominion of the Holy Spirit, the celebration of which will take place this year next May 24th, in the church at Malgre Tout, wishes through this medium to remind friends who took chances for this dominion, to discharge them in turn, especially those who are going to Madeira and who will not be here on the day of the celebration. Equally, he asks those persons who did not take chances to condescend to contribute some offering for this feast which will take place, with all pomp and decorum, on the above mentioned date.

Malgre Tout, 20th March 1874

(*The Watchman*, 24th March 1874)

New Church at Plaisance (1876)

Work on the foundations for a new church, in honour of St John the Baptist, has already begun in Plaisance. The chapel in that area is small and in bad state of repair.

Messrs Manoel Paixão de Silva, his brother Pedro da Silva, and José de Gouveia, of Plaisance, are authorized to receive donations for the above-mentioned new church, if the people of the city are generous in contributing to this project, in honour of God and the glorious St John the Baptist.

(*The Watchman, 15 September 1876*)

ADVERT
DEMERARA RAILWAY
NOTICE

Festa de Nossa Senhora do Monte, and the Celebration of the Jubilee of His Holiness the Pope at Victoria Village on SUNDAY, AUGUST 27, 1893

GRAND ILLUMINATIONS AND FIREWORKS

For the convenience of the Right Revd Dr Butler who will be accompanied by the Revd Fathers Casati and Purcell, special trains will be run as under:-

UP	AM	PM	DOWN		PM
Georgetown dep.	10:30	7:30	Mahaia dep.	noon	9:25
Belfield arr.	11:35	8:40	Belfield dep.	12:00	9:45
Do dep.		9:00	Georgetown arr.	1:00	11:00
Mahaica arr.		9:20			

Return tickets at single fares.

These Trains will stop at intermediate stations if required. The First of Decembro Band will accompany the 10:30 am train.

J W Dorman
General Manager

Georgetown Terminus
22nd August 1893

(*The Daily Liberal* 24 August 1893)

Festa do Divino Espirito Santo

No Domingo, 29 do corrente, realisa-se em Malgretout com toda a pompa e luzimento a festa do Divino Espirito Santo, constando de missa, sermão, procissão e arreial que será abrilhantado pela banda 1.º de Dezembro.

Espera-se a concorrencia de devotos áquella festa para o seu completo brilhantismo.

AGOSTINHO DE FREITAS
Imperador

Feast of the Holy Spirit

On Sunday 29th of the current month the feast of the Holy Spirit will be held at Malgretout with all pomp, and brilliance, consisting of mass, sermon, procession and decorations which will be enlivened by the popular 1st of December band.

It is hoped that this gathering of devoted persons will make such a feast a most completely brilliant one.

Agostinho De Freitas
Imperador

(*Chronica Semanal,* 14 de Maio de 1898)

Pope's Jubilee Account

In honour of the Pope's Jubilee there were celebrations on a grand scale on Sunday and yesterday amongst the Portuguese of the Colony. Shortly after dawn on Sunday morning large numbers could be seen wending their way to the Church of the Sacred Heart, Main Street, where the fete was ushered in at six am. The bells of the Church peeled forth, followed by a display of fireworks and music by the Portuguese Band. At eleven o'clock there was Pontifical High Mass which was very largely attended. At five o'clock in the afternoon service was again held, the Te Deum being sung by the choir, and the First Decembro Band playing selections of music at intervals. The porch and entrance to the church were decorated with banners and greenary. The weather being fine a large number of onlookers collected on the street close to the church to witness the celebrations.

The festivities were continued yesterday on a much larger scale than those of the previous day. The weather in the early part of the forenoon and well on to the afternoon was very unpropitious and threatened to mar the proceedings. However the maxim "things look brighter when we least expect them" was realised, for about three o'clock the dismal sky that had reigned overhead during the day disappeared and bright sunshine burst forth. The scholars attending the Portuguese College, Main Street, and the Brickdam School assembled at the Church of the Sacred Heart about three o'clock and marched to the residence of Mr J P Santos in Thomas Street, where it was arranged that the Portuguese community should assemble and afterwards proceed to the Brickdam Cathedral and thence to the Church of the Sacred Heart. The children to the number of over 100 on arriving at Mr Santos residence amused themselves by playing about the grounds, refreshments on a liberal scale being provided for them at intervals. The earliest arrivals were Bishop Butler, accompanied by Fr Scoles, who extended the children a cordial greeting. Amongst others present were Fathers Barraud, Gambetti, Moura and O'Donnell, Messrs E de M Brito Nobrego, J P Santos, Theodore D'Mattos, M Correiro, J S F Ross, A C Faria, Manoel D'Abreu, J Taxeira, A F Fernandez, M de Freitas, Antonio Gomes, J G Henriques, J Correia, J Freitas Pombo, Jose Correio, &c. Mr Santos placed the lower part of his house at the disposal of the school children, and his drawing-room for the reception of the others who took part in the proceedings. The room was nicely laid apart, seats for the Bishop and the Priests, together with the Committee, being reserved at one end, while the visitors sat around. The walls were also decorated very appropriately, a portrait of His Holiness Pope Leo XIII standing out conspicuously. When all had assembled two of the pupils of the Portuguese College stepped forward and in Portuguese language referred to the event which brought them together and thanked the Committee for having invited them to take part in the rejoicings in connection with the head of the Catholic Church. Senhor Eduardo de M Brito Nobrega, Director of the College, and the Secretary of the Jubilee Committee, also addressed those assembled referring in most appropriate terms to the reign of His Holiness. He dwelt on the temporal power of the Pope and his influence in the furtherance of Christianity as well as his exercise in the power of the Church militant here below. He concluded by saying that the mark of loyalty of the Portuguese settled in British Guiana would go forth as a testimony of their zeal in behalf of the Church to which they belonged. As the hour was getting late the Bishop did not reply, but formally thanked Mr Nobrega for the speech which he had delivered. The First Decembro Band which was present played the Portuguese National Anthem, and thereafter a procession was formed, the Band taking the lead, followed by the school children with other members of the Portuguese Community in the rear. The procession marched along Thames-Street to the Brickdam Cathedral displaying flags and banners, and the Band playing appopriate airs. The route was thronged, especially the entrance to the Cathedral, but the utmost decorum was observed. At the main entrance to the building a likeness of the Pope was placed, being ornamented round about by decorations. As the processionists passed the likeness they bowed to it, and then formed into line, the Bishop meanwhile witnessing the proceedings from the window of his residence adjacent to the Cathedral. The Band having played the Pope's hymn the procession was reformed and marched down the Brickdam and along High and Main Streets to the Church of the Sacred Heart. The line of route was crowded by onlookers, the lower order manifesting the utmost curiosity in the proceedings. The Bishop who had left his residence after the departure of the procession proceeded to a point in

Main Street where he witnessed it to the finish. But the celebrations did not end here, for in the evening one of the grandest illuminations ever witnessed in the city was displayed in front of the Church of the Sacred Heart. During the day workmen were busy arranging fairy lamps from the design of Mr C Castellani in front of the sacred edifice, while Mr Moore, of the Electric Lighting Company, was also hard at work in the erection of incandescent lamps along the buildings. Shortly after dark large crowds wended their way to the Catholic church, and took up positions on the street where a good view of the illuminations could be witnessed. About seven o'clock the lighting of the fairy lamps, which numbered over two thousand, commenced, and shortly after they were illuminated. They were of different colours, green, blue and red, and had an enchanting appearance. The Chinese lanterns of different shades which numbered close to four hundred, and which were suspended from the Church to the railing in front, and in the grounds of the Priests' residence were also lighted about eight o'clock, and lent an additional beauty and interest to the scene. But this was not all. The electric light of three hundred incandescent lamps was not put on till nine o'clock, and when the hour chimed the switch was turned on, the result being that "the scene was changed" and what before could be described as no other than beautiful bore an appearance of the finest glow. The light bursting forth like the different colours of the rainbow cast a hue along Main Street, that is rarely witnessed in the tropics, and as it died away towards midnight it left behind it the impression that the Portuguese Community of Georgetown had celebrated the fete in a style which reflected the highest credit on them. Permission to the precincts of the Church was by ticket, and those invited attended in large numbers. The First Decembro Band was present and on the stroke of nine o'clock started off with the Pope's hymn, the choir joining in the singing. Although the crowd that assembled along the streets numbered some thousands yet their behaviour was good, the police arrangements being so well arranged by acting Inspector General Wright, that not the slightest disturbance occurred. The celebrations ceased towards midnight, and shortly after the crowds dispersed to their homes. A word of praise is due to the Committee of Management, and Mr E de M Brito Nobrego, the Secretary, for the satisfactory result of their efforts.

(*The Daily Chronicle,* Tues 25 July 1893)

Pope's Jubilee in Essequibo

On Sunday, the 29th and Monday, 30th ult two important events in connection with the Roman Catholics were commemorated at the RC Church, Henrietta Village Essequibo – the Jubilee of Pope Leo 13 and the Feast of St Joseph. The Portuguese inhabitants of the Country were very enthusiastic on the occasion and decorated their stores and shops with flags, and fairy lanterns which were illuminated for the occasion. The interior of the Chapel was tastefully decorated with flowers and plants. Father Van Newton was the only officiating Priest, and preached both morning and evening on Sunday, appropriate Sermons to the occasion. There was not a single case of disorderly conduct reported amongst the Portuguese.

(*The Daily Chronicle,* Thurs, 2 Nov 1893)

East Coast

Thursday being the eve of John the Baptist the Portuguese in the different villages made large bonfires at their doors in the evening.

(*The Reflector* 25 June, 1892)

Plaisance – Authorities object to bon-fires

"The Portuguese have a habit of burning barrels, boxes, etc in the night on the public road whenever the feasts of St John and St Peter come around. They followed the custom a few weeks ago on the occasion of St John's feast, and two men were summoned before the Magistrate by the police for it. They were reprimanded and discharged. This, I suppose, will put a stop to what is a nuisance, as the smoke, sparks and heat from these bonfires cause a deal of discomfort to the public.

(*The Daily Chronicle* 14 July, 1898)

VESPERA DE S. JOÃO BAPTISTA

MAGNÍFICA EXCURSÃO AO LUAR PARA BELFIELD,
NA NOITE DE 23 DO CORRENTE,
EM LEMBRANÇA D'AQUELLE GRANDE SÃO JOÃO
BAPTISTA.

O comboio partirá de Georgetown pelas 7 horas e meia da noite e parará na Plaisance, Beterverwagting e Buxton para tomar passageiros, devendo chegar a Belfield pelas 8 horas e um quarto.

Accompanhara este Comboio uma Banda de Musica.

O ex.ᵐᵒ snr. Luiz Fernandes dignou conceder aos promotores d'esta excursão o uso do Hypodromo de Belfield. N'este vastissimo terreno tocará uma bem composta banda de musica, e haverá uma grande exhibição de fogo artificial. Os excursionistas, em mostrando os seus bilhetes, tem entrada gratis. Os de primeira classe poderão ter assentos reservados.

Aquelles que tem saudades de nossa querida Madeira de certo não deixarão de tomar vantagem d'esta esplendida diversão em honra de São João.

Mãos á obra, pois. Deitemos as nossas sortes, compremos os nossos bilhetes e seguimos para Belfield para passar uma tão bellissima noite de borga.

Os promotores farão todo o possivel de accomodar todos aquelles que os coadjuvarem n'esta empreza.

A volta de Belfield será pelas 11 horas.

Refrescos de primeira qualidade a preços rasoaveis.

Bilhetes acham-se á venda na loja de Smith Brothers & Ca. e na Estação do Railway.

PREÇO DE BILHETES D'IDA E VOLTA:

De Georgetown	...	...96 Cts.	72 Cts.
„ Plaisance		...84 „	60 „
„ Beterverwagting		...72 „	48 „
„ Buxton	...	...60 „	40 „

VESPERS OF ST JOHN THE BAPTIST
MAGNIFICENT MOONLIGHT EXCURSION TO BELFIELD
ON THE NIGHT OF THE 23rd OF THE PRESENT MONTH
In Memory of The Great St John The Baptist

The train will leave Georgetown at 7:30 pm and will stop at Plaisance, Beterverwagting and Buxton to take on passengers and is due to arrive at Belfield at 8:15.

A Musical Band will be on the train.

Mr Luiz Fernandes has been kind enough to grant the use of the Hypodrome at Belfield to the promoter of this excursion. In this very large area an excellent band will play and there will be a big firework display. The excursionists will have free entrance on presentation of their tickets. First class passengers can have reserved seats.

Those who miss our beloved Madeira will surely take advantage of this splendid outing in honour of St John.

Don't be left out. Come on then, let us take a chance, buy our tickets and head for Belfield to spend a most beautiful night of fêting.

The promoters will do everything to accommodate those who cooperate in their venture.

The return from Belfield will be at 11:00 pm.

First class refreshments at reasonable prices.

Tickets on sale at Smiths' Brothers shop and at the railway Station.

Prices for Return Tickets

From Georgetown.	96 cts	72 cts
From Plaisance	84 cts	60 cts
From Beterverwagting.	72 cts	48 cts
From Buxton.	60 cts	40 cts

(*Chronica Semanal,* 15 June 1898)

Church Feast Day
East Bank

The feast of the Blessed Virgin was celebrated at Meadow Bank Roman Catholic Church on Sunday. Inside the church was decorated with banners, buntings and flags, while the altar was beautifully adorned with floral decorations. The Church premises on the east have been cleared, and the procession took place entirely in the church yard, proceeding twice around the building. The route of the procession was decorated with garlands, flags and bunting, and crossed by arches of which they were not less than twenty-eight. The procession was led by a cross-bearer and two altar boys with lights after whom followed the school children. The girls wearing wreaths and regalia, the women of the Blessed Virgin Society wearing nets on the heads and regalias, and various men's societies attired in red, purple and blue, the young men of the St Aloysius Guild, the altar boys, the celebrant, Father Victorine, and the band. In it were four banners also and five statues representative of St Peter, St John, St Joseph and the Blessed Virgin with the infant, the last being resplendent in shining blue and white gold stars and art work and silver crown on the head which unfortunately in returning to the church was knocked off and occupied the sexton a few minutes in refixing. This done the choir and band rendered two pieces and Father Victorine brought the celebration to a close.

(*The Daily Chronicle,* Tues 26 August, 1902)

Feast of Saint Philomena

The feast to commemorate the first centenary of the findings of the relics of St Philomena, Virgin and Martyr, was observed at the Church of the Sacred Heart, Main Street, on Sunday. Preliminary to the feast, special services were held on the three preceding days. On Thursday at 5:30 pm the inauguration ceremony of the new chapel was laid on the 19th July, 1901, by His Lordship, Bishop Galton, then Vicar General. The chapel is erected on the south side of the church, the work being done under the supervision of the architect, Mr C Castellani, late of the Public works Department. The chapel is simple but elegant; and although not quite completed inwardly, it has cost $2,400. To finish it $600 will be necessary.

At the inauguration ceremony a procession of the members of St Philomena Society, all young ladies, was formed for the purpose of transporting the large image of the saint from her old altar on the north east side of the church to the chapel. The procession moved to the strains of the Portuguese Primeiro de Dezembro Band playing the hymn of the Saint, the members joining in the chorus. This service was concluded with special invocations, a sermon by Father Justino and the Benediction by Father Gambetti.

At 7 pm on Friday there was Solemn Novena in honour of the Saint, a Sermon and Benediction.

On Saturday at the 7 am Mass there was the general communion of the members, terminating with Novena, Sermon and Benediction.

The Solemn feast was celebrated on the Sunday. At the 7 am Mass all those devoted to the Saint took Holy Communion. There was Solemn High Mass at 11 am, the celebrant being the Bishop-elect, Fathers Gambetti and Victorine, acting as Deacon and Sub-deacon respectively. The Sermon on the life and good example of the Saint was preached by Fr Justino, the Director of the Society.

The afternoon service began at 4 o'clock with the intoning of Solemn Vespers by the Bishop, clergy, acolytes and choir. Then followed a small procession of three poor girls, dressed in white, led by six little angels, and accompanied by the band. The procession started from the Sacristy and went through the main door of the Church to the big altar. The outfits of these poor girls were provided from the funds of the Society. Seventy five new members were then consecrated, and Father Justino again preached.

The scene of the afternoon was the grand procession which came out of the main entrance of the Church wending its way through the north gate to High Street, into the Covent of Mercy gate, traversing the Church grounds, and the Presbytery yard, onto High Street into the north gate again, and thence through the main door of the Church. The societies represented were the Blessed Sacrament (men with scarlet capes); our Lady (men with blue and white capes); St Joseph (men with red and white capes); St Aloysius (ladies with blue and white regalia and medals); the children of Mary (boys with red and white tassels regalias extending from breast to shoulder); St Philomena (young ladies dressed in white, with wreaths, veils and scarlet ribbons); Infant Jesus (little girls in white wearing wreaths and blue ribbons). The Bishop served by Father Gambetti and Victoriane and the acolytes brought up the rear of the procession followed by the band, playing a slow march. The beautiful standards of the different Societies, embroidered in gold and silver, were carried by the members, but conspicuous was the spledid image of Saint Philomena lying in her sepulchre under a canopy of structural work and borne on the shoulders of four men of the St Joseph Society. There were about 400 young ladies of the society present in church, and as the image passed them they showered flowers over it. This service closed with the Benediction of the Blessed Sacrament, pronounced by the Bishop.

The church internally was very attractive and beautiful. Bunting, festoons drapery, artificial and real flowers etc were in evidence. The High Altar was all that could be desired. Huge brass candlesticks, vases and images etc were to be seen here and there, and when the electric and candle lights were put on, the church looked very beautiful.

Special mention should be made of the chapel of St Philomena. It was decorated with garlands and strings of artificial flowers and veiling, the standing image resting on the altar surrounded with a large quantity of sweet flowers.

The exterior of the church was prettily and tastefully decorated with flags, panorama balls, crotons, strings of crotons running from pole to pole, arches etc. The choir under the conductorship of Signor Castellani, gave a good account of itself, many pieces rendered being of a modern type and very much appreciated. The "Primeiro de Decembro" Band under the baton of Senhor V X de Silva, supplied suitable music throughout the feast. It must be mentioned that the expense of erecting the chapel was met by the Portuguese of Georgetown, the Demerarans of Funchal, Madeira, and the *AÇORIANOS* of Boston and New Bedford USA.

Great credit is due to Father Justino for the zeal and interest he has taken in the completion of the chapel. The many improvements he has effected in the working of the church societies and the changes he has made in the church functions with the sanction of his superior, Father Gambetti, speak volumes in his favour.

(*The Daily Chronicle,* Tues 2 September 1902)

Novena Mass

The traditional Christmas Novena which has become part of our country's Catholic life, has always been observed at the church. The Novena Mass was originally at 4am with the church opened from 3am. It was moved to 5 am. . . . With the beginning of the Evening Mass Sacred Heart church began the Evening Novena Mass at 7 o'clock . . .

Bells

Again it was at Christmas Midnight Mass in 1905 that the church's familiar peal of bells rang out for the first time with the *Gloria in Excelsis* . . . Total peal of ten bells weighs over 8,000 lbs – the largest the Angelus Bell – over one ton. Made in West Troy, USA. Church declared National Shrine of the Sacred Heart – Feb 1960 for British Guiana.

(*Catholic Standard,* Christmas 1961)

Bemdetto

"This is a special Christmas Novena which takes place in all the churches, and is of Portuguese origin. In every church there is a very early Mass during which the traditional "Bemdetto" is sung and a sermon preached. The churches are crowded for these Novena Masses – a fitting way of concentrating devotion on *Christ* and his *Mass.* So long as it thrives, there will be no one in the Colony who will be able to regard Christmas merely as a public holiday."

(*Missionary Magazine,* Vol. 1, No. 2. April 1935, p. 45)

Malgretout – in spite of all

Malgretout is true to its name. *In spite of all* manner of difficulties it is managing to carry on. Situated on the West Bank of Rio Demerara this country Mission is one of the oldest in the colony. The village, where the presbytery and church are situated, is but a shadow of its former glory. Once thickly populated by good old Madeirans, staunch and generous Catholics, their numbers have now divided into a miserable fraction. Their present number can be counted on the fingers of one hand. The churches have lost all their splendour and glory. Once the pride of the whole country district which extends for miles and miles, they are now silent proofs to all passers-by of a poverty-stricken area.

(*Missionary Magazine,* Vol. 2. No. 9. January 1937, p.16)

Statue of Our Lady of Fatima
Sacred Heart Church, 1950

The Portuguese in Guyana have great devotion to Our Lady of Fatima who appeared at Fatima, Portugal in 1917.

Sacred Heart Church, Main Street, was the scene of many colourful and devotional May Processions in honour of Our Lady of Fatima in the 1950s and 1960s.

The Cultural Contribution of the Portuguese

Significant though the economic and religious contributions of the Portuguese were to the country their cultural contributions should not be overlooked nor down-played. Unfortunately, the little known history of the Portuguese in British Guiana stressed only their economic progress. The newspapers of the day are replete with lengthy and detailed descriptions of concerts, dramatic recitals and dramatic plays performed by Portuguese artistes as well as the performances of a few Portuguese bands.

In the post mid-nineteenth century the British Guianese were very much attuned to the delights of the arts of music, drama and poetry. The Portuguese with their inherited love for music where not only on the *festas* but during the harvesting and crushing of the grapes, the cutting of the canes, they loved to sing and dance. It will be recalled in the early days of their arrival in Demerara that, though they brought with them few possessions, they brought their *rajão* (type of banjo). So it should come as no surprise that the Portuguese established musical bands, among them the most popular – the "Primeiro de Dezembro" band established in 1879 under very talented conductors. This band, together with the British Guiana Militia Band, played at many important functions. The Portuguese distinguished themselves also in dramatic productions and sacred and secular musical concerts of a high standard. Even young boys performed most creditably on the *braggas* (small Portuguese guitar) in the Estudiantina String Band.

Balls given by the Portuguese at the Assembly Rooms excited the envy of their English friends because of their grand style. One of the highlights of Portuguese cultural events was the celebration in 1898 of the 400th Anniversary of Vasco de Gama's opening of the sea route to India.

The two accounts given in *The Echo* and *The Daily Chronicle* express the pride of the Portuguese in their historical heritage. An off-shoot of these extravagant celebrations were the unique cyclists' parade with the creatively decorated cycles and the subsequent forming of a Vasco da Gama Cycling Club – raising cycling to a professional sport in Guyana.

The Portuguese were no less active in the educational and professional fields; they listed among their ranks doctors, lawyers, auditors, diplomats and others. Though they ventured late into the politial arena – the Hon Francis Dias was the first Portuguese in the Legislative council in the 1920s – they served as Mayors and Town Councillors in Georgetown and New Amsterdam and were extremely active in village politics to say nothing of serving as Directors on the Boards of many companies. In the 1860s Dr Manget winning a seat in the College of Electors had advised the Portuguese "not to meddle with politics on this or any other occasion." They obviously took his advice very much to heart.

The excerpt of the wedding of J P Santos, one of the leading Portuguese businessmen of his day, illustrates the panache and elegance with which the Portuguese graced such occasions. The short sketch of José Gomes D'Aguiar in his obituary described him as one of the richest, if not the richest businessman in British Guiana. They served in high diplomatic positions and were not averse to voicing their views on the issues of the day. Mr L R Andrade, a gifted linguist and Venezuelan consul involved in negotiations in the British Guiana-Venezuala Boundary dispute, a director of quite a few companies, was an especially vitriolic writer as the excerpt from his letter on "Excise and Rum Duties" blatantly illustrates. The Portuguese press in the colony, *A União Portugueza, O Voz Portuguez, Chronica Semanal* and the *Watchman* were not behind the times in expressing their views.

Above all, the Portuguese gave much time and attention to caring for their poor and sick. It should be noted that religious celebrations were not only devoted to the sacred but to the very secular and practical expressions of their faith when food and clothing were shared out to the needy in honour of some feast day. To ensure that there be regular donations and continued care the Portuguese Benevolent Society was formed in 1875 – the main object "the encouragement of industry and charity among the Members."

It is especially noteworthy that as a mark of solidarity with their African brethren the Portuguese designated in 1899 the anniversary of emancipation day a HOLY DAY.

"Portuguese Benevolent Society of British Guiana"

EDITORIAL

"Our Portuguese readers will learn with much satisfaction that The Bill to incorporate the *Portuguese Benevolent Society of British Guiana* has been passed as ordinance No. 5 of 1875, yesterday the 27 May 1875. The purposes of the Society are very excellent and if it continues to receive the support hitherto accorded there is little doubt that the Colonial Government will have no Portuguese among the inmates of the *Alms house.* It will be a just source of pride to our Portuguese fellow Colonists to be able to assert and prove that Portuguese do not require aid from the colonial funds apported for the support of paupers. It will be also a living indicator of the industry and intrinsic worth of Lusitania's sons, who came hither, hardly a quarter of a century ago, destitute of every outward means to the attainment of wealth and happiness. There are several wealthy Portuguese among its members and we direct their special attention to the preamble of the ordinance which declares that the funds of the Society will be raised by subscription, *with* or without *the aid of donations.* The object of the Society is the promotion of the work of Charity. Let the wealthy members give generously as with an open hand. Omitted they can give sufficient to form a permanent fund from which a constant revenue will flow. For the honour of Portugal we beseech them not to desert the Society but to aid, foster and advance it in every way. Let them vie with each other in rich, substantial donation, and their name will go down to posterity inscribed on the records of the Society in letters of gold. To each wealthy member we say, put down *one* thousand dollars as a foundation gift to be invested in Bank Shares or Colonial Bonds. To the fair daughters of *Lusitania,* single and married, we say that they too will find ample scope for woman's ministering care in the welfare of the sick. Visit the sick of the Society, administer those comforts so grateful and necessary to the sick, and by reading good books help to shorten the long and weary hours of pain. We hope the Portuguese of British Guiana will not disgrace the country by neglecting the Society, and we wish it wealth, success and prosperity."

(*The Watchman,* Friday, May 28 1875)

Schedule I
LIST OF FOUNDERS

1 Querino Pompilio
2 Alexandre A d'Andrade
3 Antonio Joaquim
4 Calisto José Nunes
5 José A Machado Pacheco
6 Lucio J Jardin Camara
7 José Martins
8 Ricardo José Gonsalves
9 Manoel Pereira Jorge
10 Vincente Xavier da Silva
11 Julio de Freitas
12 Joao Augusto Cunha
13 José Calisto Nunes
14 Sergio Auguste d'Araujo
15 Guilherme A Comacho
16 Joao Gomes Henriques
17 Joao Leonidio de Freitas
18 Manoel Gomes Loija
19 Antonio Marques Gonsalves
20 Miquel Rodrigues dos Santos
21 Maximiano José Bettencourt
22 Izedoro Leandro F Jardim
23 Manoel Nunes
24 Luiz Gonsalves de Freitas
25 Manoel de Paiva
26 José dos Ramos
27 José Rodrigues
28 Augusto Cesar de Faria
29 Antonio Rodrigues Vallado
30 Dr M H S Pereira

31 Antonio Venancio Jardim Camara
32 Augusto Rodrigues
33 Manoel Mendes
34 Antonio Gonsalves Ferreira
35 José Ignacio
36 Profirio d'Oliveira
37 Francisco Narciso de Freitas
38 José Augusto dos Santos
39 Francisco Baptista
40 Domingos C F Ramalho
41 Ricardo Cunha, jr
42 Joao d'Agrella
43 Manoel Rodrigues de Sousa
44 Clemente Joaquim de Sousa
45 André Sabino
46 Luiz A Monteiro Cabral
47 Antonio Archanjo Rodrigues
48 Constantino A Mattos
49 Augusto Joao Cunha
50 Vincente Julio d'Araujo
51 José Gomes d'Aguiar
52 Manoel Fernandes
53 Manoel Sardinda
54 Feliciano Gomes de Faria
55 Manoel de Sousa Coelho
56 Francisco Gonsalves Quinta
57 Manoel d'Oliveira, jr
58 Rufino Joao Vieira

Schedule II

BY-LAWS FOR THE CONSTITUTION, GOVERNMENT AND MANAGEMENT OF THE PORTUGUESE BENEVOLENT SOCIETY OF BRITISH GUIANA

Objects of the Society

1. The encouragement of industry and charity among the Members.

2. The relief of Members in sickness, or in case of inability to work from old age, or of imprisonment, not under any sentence for felony or misdemeanour, or in case of inability to obtain employment, or to acquire the necessary means of subsistence: Provided always that in case any Member shall allege his inability to procure work, he shall prove to the Board of Directors that he has done all in his power to obtain employment and has failed to obtain any.

3. To provide money for the suitable funeral expenses, and the decent burial of Members when requested so to do by the famlies or representatives of the deceased.

4. To afford relief to the Widows and Orphans of Members whenever the Board of Directors shall be satisfied that the said Widows and Orphans are really in need of such relief.

5. To establish, as soon as the Funds of the Society will permit, Schools for the education of children of Members of the Society.

Constitution of the Society

1. The Society shall be exclusively composed of Portuguese of the Male sex, or their Male descendants, and every Member shall contribute weekly the sum of one shilling.

2. Every Candidate for admission to the Society must be a person of good character.

3. He must not be over Fifty years of age at the time of his admission: But the founders of the Society shall be exempt from the qualification as to age. In proof whereof the Candidate shall produce his Baptismal Certificate, or if unable to do so, a Certificate of his age from the Board of Administration.

4. He must not be labouring, at the time of his admission, under any disease disabling him from work, and must prove such freedom from disease by the Certificate to that effect of the Society's Medical Prac-

tioner or of any other duly qualified Practitioner if the Society's Medical Practitioner cannot act.

5. Any person who applies for admission as a Member of the Society shall produce to the Board of Administrators the above-mentioned Certificates and inform the said Board of his wish to be a Member of the Society and the said Board after examining the said Certificates may either upon personal knowledge or information supplied by other Members admit or reject the person so applying for admission.

6. A book shall be kept as Register of Members belonging to the Society and in it shall be written the name, age, occupation, property or income, parentage and residence of each Member of the Society.

7. To each new Member on Registration shall be given a printed Certificate of admission and a copy of the By-Laws of the Society. This printed Certificate of admission shall contain the name of such Member together with the date of his registration as Member of the Society. The said printed Certificate of admission shall be signed by the Board of Directors, and for such Certificate the new Member shall pay two shillings in addition to his entrance Fee of twenty shillings. The sum of two shillings to be paid for the said printed Certificate of admission must be paid on delivery of the Certificate to the Member.

8. The entrance Fee of a Member shall be twenty shillings, and in case any Member be unable to pay the said entrance Fee in full on admission he may in such case pay one half on admission and five months shall be allowed him for payment of the balance in monthly instalments of two shillings each.

9. No Fee shall be chargeable for the copy of the By-Laws to be delivered to a Member on admission.

Duties of Members.

10. Every member of the Society shall be bound to attend the Society's meetings in clean respectable clothing and to conduct himself in private as well as in public as a decent, orderly, moral member of a Christian community should.

11. Every member must pay regularly his aforesaid weekly contribution to the Society.

Grand Concert of Sacred Music

MISS DeVASCONCELLOS has the honour to announce that she will give a GRAND CONCERT of SACRED MUSIC in the Assembly Rooms on the evening of Monday next, the 8th instant; where she will be assisted by Miss MARY AMALIA De VASCONCELLOS, DR BECKER and MR D VIEIRA.

The Militia Band will be in attendance.

1st PART

1. Introduction by the Band
2. Qual Giglio Candido, Solo from Mercadante
        (by Miss Mary Christina De Vasconcellos)
3. Loetantum Coch – Solo Offertorie
        (by Miss Mary Amalia De Vasconcellos)
4. Duo, Flute and Piano –
        (Mr Vieira and Dr Becker)
5. Ego, Sum panis, Duetto Battorglia
        (by the Two Sisters)
6. Finale of the 1st Part by the Band

2nd PART

1. Introduction by the Band
2. Cujus animan, Solo from Rossini
        (by Miss M C De Vasconcellos)
3. Quittollis, Solo – Capocci
        (by Miss M A De Vasconcellos)
4. Duo, Flute and Piano
        (by Mr Vieira and Dr Becker)
5. Qui Sedet, Duetto – Terziani
        (by the Two Sisters)
6. Finale of the 2nd Part by the Band

GOD SAVE THE QUEEN!
Admission – 4 Shillings
To Commence at 8.

(*The Colonist,* Tues 2 March 1869)

Portuguese Amateurs Give Entertainment

A very lively Dramatic and Musical Entertainment by Portuguese Amateurs will be given in the Philharmonic Hall on Wednesday next in aid of the Building Fund of the Catholic Church now in the course of erection at Meadow Bank. Several popular Musical Selections and a couple of One Act Comedies will be given.

Senhor Cezar Castellani will be the conductor, and the Militia Band will give their services.

(The Watchman, Friday 26 November 1876)

Bandmaster Appointed for Primeiro de Dezembro Band

Senhor João Nobrega de Noronha, late Bandmaster of the "Recreio dos Lavradores" Band, Camara dos Lobos, Madeira, has been appointed bandmaster of the "Premeiro de Dezembro" band of the city established in 1876. Senhor Noronha is a talented musician and plays flute, clarionet, violin, piano, etc. We wish the "Primeiro de Dezembro" all success under his able tuition.

Concert by the Primerio de Dezembro in the Promenande Gardens

The following is the programme of music to be discoursed at the Promenade Gardens tonight at 8 o'clock by the Portuguese "Primeiro de Dezembro" Band under the direction of Senhor Nobrega:-

PART I

1. Slow March . . . . A Portugueza . . . .
2. Spanish Valse . . . . Santiago . . . . A Corbin
3. Fantasia . . . . Rose d'Amour . . . . Bleger
4. Polka . . . . Kermess . . . . Faust

PART II

1. Valse . . . . Heather Blossoms . . . J Robinson
1. Mazurka . . . . Stella . . . . A Neuparth
3. Quadrille . . . . St Domingo . . . . G Webb
4. Galop . . . . Holiday . . . . Miller

GOD SAVE THE QUEEN

(The Daily Chronicle, Wednesday, 25 January 1893)

BANDA PORTUGUEZA – Fundon-se nesta cidade, no começ d'este mez, uma banda de musica portugueza composta na mor parte de membros da associação de beneficencia. For dado á nora banda o titulo de – *Philarmonica Primeiro de Dezembro* – por ter sido installada no dia anniversario em que Portugal se libertou de jugo castellano. A commissão nomeada para dirigir esta sociedade trabalha com actividade e exforça – se quanto e possivel para que tao util quao proveitosa instituição de desenvolva quanto antes. Secundo parece a ordem para a compra dos instrumentos deve hir para a Europa no proximo paquete.

Translation:

PORTUGUESE BAND – At the beginning of this month, a Portuguese musical band, mainly comprising members of the charitable association, was formed in this city. The new band was given the name – *1st December Philharmonic* – since it was installed on the anniversary of the day on which Portugal was freed from Castillian oppression.

The commission nominated to head this society is actually working and doing as much as possible so that such a useful and beneficial organization develops more than ever before. Accordingly, it appears than an order for the purchase of instruments should go to Europe on the next boat.

(*The Watchman,* 8 December 1876)

Plaisance Musical Band

From what we hear, the little musical band, or some such thing, which was formed by the Portuguese some months ago in the town of Plaisance, is going to Capoy on Saturday 29th of this month, apparently to play at the feast which is being celebrated there on the following day.

The musicians of the band have already made high split hats to make their debut on that day.

(*The Watchman,* 21 September 1877)

Portuguese Consul

Manoel Fernandes Camacho – appointed consul for HM the King of Portugal in British Guiana and Consul General for the West Indies – appointment met with great satisfaction in Madeira. *O DIREITO*, 28th October 1877 "Our countryman, Mr Manoel F Camacho, proprietor and merchant in Georgetown. That gentleman is already the agent in Demerara of the Bank of Portugal, Commercial Bank of Madeira, and the Bank of Lisbon and the Azores. The nomination is a good one. Mr Camacho has been one among those from Madeira residing in Demerara who has rendered the greatest service to his countrymen.

On Wed 28th Nov nuptials of M F Camacho – Consul General son of our highly respectable proprietor to Christina Izabel, second daughter of *José Gomes D'Aguiar,* Esquire, in R C Cathedral by Bishop Etheridge – given away by honourable father, Senhor Francisco F Camacho.

(*Watchman,* 30 November, 1877)

Private Flag of Merchant

Mrs Rosa Fernades, mother of Mr John Fernandes, merchant in city, died in Madeira aged 90. Mr Fernandes' private flag was hoisted half mast high at the Tower.

(*The Daily Chronicle,* Sun 3 September 1882)

Hospital for Portuguese Benevolent Society

A rumour is in circulation that the Portuguese Benevolent society seriously entertains the project of purchasing the Caledonian Hotel buildings, with a view of converting them into a hospital for the treatment of sick members of the organization.

(*Dem Daily Chronicle,* Wednesday 6 December 1882)

HOSPITAL OF ST LUKE

HOSPITAL DE S. LUCAS.

ESTE ESTABELECIMENTO SITUADO

NA ESQUINA DE PRINCESS E HIGH STREETS.

GEORGETOWN

Offerece aos doentes d'ambos os sexos todas as Commodidades e comfórtos d'uma casa particular.

Acha-se provido com quartos particulares tanto para homens como para senhoras :

CONDIÇÕES DE TRATAMENTO

1ª Classe em quarto particular $10 por semana.

2ª Classe na enfermaria $7 por semana.

CONSULTAS INCLUINDO REMEDIOS 60 CENTS.

O preço para operações cirurgicas depende da natureza e gravidade dellas.

DEMERARA 1 de Outubro de 1897.

HOSPITAL OF ST LUKE

This establishment is situated at the corner of Princess & High Streets,

GEORGETOWN

Offers to sick persons of both sexes all the conveniences and comforts of a private home

It is provided with private rooms for men as well as for women:

CONDITIONS OF TREATMENT

1st Class in a private room $10 per week

2nd Class in a ward $7 per week

Consultations include medications 60 cents.

The cost for surgical operations depends on the nature and gravity of the illness

Demerara, 1 October 1897

(*Chronica Semnal,* 13 October 1897)

The Portuguese Benevolent Society

Formation of a New Society.

A meeting of the members of the extinct Portuguese Benevolent Society was convened at the Society's Hall in Robb Street, on the 23rd ult at 3 o'clock for the object of raising the society under different government and new laws. About 150 members were present and Mr Manoel Gonsalves presided. He explained to the members in a few words that the object of that meeting was to look after the foundation of the Benevolent Society between the members who belonged to the extinct Portuguese Benevolent Society of British Guiana and who were in possession of their rights on the 4th July, last. He went on to say further that those members who had been dismissed should have the right to settle their arrears in order to possess identical rights with the other members. This proposal was approved by the majority, and the new Society was denominated "The Portuguese Benevolent Fraternity Society". A committee consisting of the Chairman Messrs Augusto C de Faria, M F Menzes, João Gomes Henriques, José Martins, Luiz M Leal and José A Machado Pacheco, was appointed, to elaborate the statues. The immovable property of the Portuguese Benevolent Society after the payment of the widow's pensions and other expense is about twelve thousand dollars.

(*Demerara Daily Chronicle (Mail Edition)*) Saturday December 10, 1887

Society Dona Maria Pia

To the editor – Daily Chronicle

In the business of the Court of Policy of Friday last, I noticed under the heading of Friendly Societies, that a petition from a certain Portuguese Society denominated DONA MARIA PIA has been laid over through the Hon B Howell Jones, together with a copy of the rules of that society. Before such rules may be approved, and before such a society may be incorporated by the Legislature, I beg leave to inform the honourable members of the Court of Policy that the statement of the Dona Maria Pia being the outcome of the failure of the long existing Portuguese Benevolent Society of British Guiana is quite erroneous.

The Old Benevolent Society, as it is termed never ended in failure at all, but was simply allowed to remain at a stand-still in order to get off its shoulders the great amount of pensions that were due to the numerous widows &c. and after the clearances of such pensions &c, there will then be continued the identical society with the same members.

The Committee in charge of paying the aforesaid widows, &c have ended their arduous task, and the society has since the 8th inst, assumed a flourishing position under the name of the Benevolent Society *Fraternidade Portugueza of British Guiana* and is already under new rules approved by a good majority of members. These rules will be as early as possible presented to the Honourable Court of Policy in order to obtain the incorporation of the Society.

I beg to inform the Honourable members in conclusion that the Dona Maria Pia Society has nothing to do with the Benevolent Society Fraternidade Portugueza of British Guiana. These two societies are as much strangers, to each other as a Chinese is to a Barbadian.

I am Sir &C

Pro Bono Publico

Georgetown December 19th, 1887

(*The Daily Chronicle,* Wednesday 21 December, 1887)

The Portuguese as Colonists – 1890 June 19th

The Portuguese are with few exceptions Catholics. Their love for their church is plainly seen in their self denial and their strict observances of feasts, fasts, and days of obligation. Now there are many Protestants who regard a Portuguese Catholic as of little worth because he is so un-English in his birth and religion, but that is a mistake that is so common that custom has taught us to make light of it.

Many people thought on the arrival of the Governor to the colony because he is a Catholic that all Portuguese would have free entrance to Government House and that the priests of the church would have sat like rulers of the land. In both of these expectations these people have been disappointed. Perhaps if the Protestant Community had understood the opinions of the Lord Gormanston of the Portuguese Community they would not have been so hasty in their conclusions.

Lord Gormanston is one who gives merit where it is deserved all things being equal, but a greater mistake could never be made than the fancy that because the Portuguese as a body are the most wealthy citizens that it is His Excellency's desire to make them rulers of the land. On the contrary he thinks they pay too much attention to their business and that it would be impossible to wash them away from this object to become legislators, and in certain remarks said by His Excellency we have learnt that he regretted to see the people who were so industrious so utterly devoid of true ambition with very few exceptions.

However kindly the editor of the "Echo" might be disposed towards us we very much regret the vein that led him on in his reform article of Wednesday last week (Wed 9th July, 1890).

Whatever the editor means by "reform" it is plain that he is cut to the quick in disappointment and it would have been better for him to have expected nothing for then he would not have been disappointed. The reform programmed has not yet seen the light, we have little interest in it at the best, but the editor of the Echo whose soul will not stand the impudence of the present constitution, thinks it is full time for "gill pots" to turn up, and we conclude that unable to wait any longer on the slow way that the Government is proceeding to bring about reform. He must have enquired of the "witch" who has told him of the constitution of the colony as ammended will consist of the following terms in the main.

The inhabitants of the Colony will be directly represented by eight members. There will be checkmated by eight officials and the Governor, the latter to have a casting vote. The qualification of an elective member is $10.000 dollars. What are we as Portuguese to do with the modelling of a constitution which promises us nothing in return. Even those who have been agitating for a new constitution have seen too plainly that while they have been asking for bread, it is just possible that all they will get is just a stone.

Our friend the Echo, who certainly may lay claim to be an active mover in the Confederate Campaign might settle himself down to his special pleading, and don't for one moment imagine that the Portuguese wish to be encumbered with the burden of the state even though they happen to possess the qualifications which those who are made for reform would not possess with the limited measures that has extended them. There must be a line somewhere and if the qualifications for elective member were placed as low as $500, there are too many who are clamouring for return and would like to sit in the highest places would not have the necessary qualifications.

We care not to transport to our columns the honourable mention of the Governor that the Echo has been pleased to place on record, but regret that the editor should have found it necessary to open his vials of wrath on a matter which he has drawn from his imagination.

As Portuguese we are not unmindful of our duty as citizens and although it has been too plainly evident that the treatment we have received of late from the government has not been such as we had a right to expect yet, we prefer to be beholders of all that passes and perhaps we will not always happened that "When rogues fall out" honest men come into their rights.

(*A União Portugueza*, Sabado 7 Junho 1890)

Portuguese Exhibit at World's Fair, Chicago

Agricultural Building Unique – 107 varieties of useful woods, among them greeheart and mora . . .

A very fine assortment of art-needlework by the Portuguese colonists of Guiana of featherwork in fans and flowers, of fish-scale and fibre work and of ornamented inlaid work in work boxes and tables, illustrate some of the manufactured productions which a large series of photographs of people and places and water colour sketches of the scenery of the little known interior, gives an idea of the physical aspect of Guiana.

(*The Daily Liberal,* 2 July, 1893)

Ball At Assembly Rooms

(by a Special Correspondent)

The Ball referred to in the columns of the *Daily Liberal* a fortnight ago, is now a thing of the past, and I am enabled to give an account of the festivities that took place within the walls of the spacious Hall at the Assembly Rooms on Monday night. It may not be generally known that the 5th June is one of those days in the year that is annually kept up at

Funchal, with the greatest pomp and ceremony obtainable in that Island Madeira, which was termed by one of the eminent Portuguese writers as the "Flower of the Ocean". Our Portuguese citizens having still within their breast a patriotic affection for their native land, have for the second time in this Colony, kept up the day by getting up a Subscription Ball among those of their nationality. The Ball was formerly opened at 9pm on the arrival of Dr de Mello, the Portuguese Consul for Demerara, who drove up at the hour mentioned in full state uniform, accompanied by Dr P de Mello, his lady. Dancing commenced at 9.15 sharp, and was kept up until the wee sma' hours, the invities having left for their homes at 3.30 am. A sumptuous supper was served at 12.30, the Consul presiding, and Senhor Commendoder Manoel Gonsalves, Merchant and Mr José Francisco de Freitas, Merchant also, sitting at the presidential table, and among them were also Portuguese elite of our community. The Consul gave an instructive address, explaining to his subjects the day they were celebrating, and concluded by proposing the health of D Carlos and D Maria Amelia, the Portuguese King and Queen; to which Mr Jorge Camacho the chairman of the Ball replied in appropriate terms, proposing the health of their representative in this Colony Dr De Mello, and her ladyship D P De Mello. At the western side of the table, (the Consul having sat the eastern side), there were to be seen Messrs M L Da Costa, Manoel Correiro, Theo A D'Mattos, John Correa, Barrister, M Correa, J G Henriques, and many other gentlemen too numerous to mention, with their respective ladies. Mr D'Mattos delivered a short speech. He said it was a pleasure to him and it must be a pleasure to all assembled there that evening celebrating an event which at that very moment·was also being celebrated with great pomp in their native land Madeira, and in saying so, he remarked that they were not partaking alone in these festivities, but the Danish people were also celebrating that day, it being their country's national day, and further that at Chicago, USA as could be seen from the WI&P telegram, the 5th June was this year declared a fete day. They had to be thankful to Mr L Da Costa, the energetic secretary who spared no time to give them what he termed a high class celebration, which was unequalled in the annals of Guiana, in so far as their countrymen were concerned, and he concluded by proposing the health of the King and Queen of Portugal, also of their representative in

Demerara, Dr D'Mello, and the committee entrusted with the Management of the grand affair. Mr M L Da Costa replied thanking the company for their kind attention, but he regretted to say that no one there sitting at that table, was aquainted with the history of their country; and could not explain what was being celebrated on that day; and the company dispersed dancing being resumed, as I have said, until the early hours of the morn. The wines and other delicacies were first class and better could not be desired. There end a true account of the 5th June ball given by our Portuguese friends, and we trust they in the near future see their way in inviting their English and other friends with whom they associate in their daily business to partake of their festivities.

[5th June 1834 – Constitutional Charter proclaimed in Madeira]

(*The Daily Liberal,* Wed, 7 June 1893)

Death of J G D'Aguiar – June 2 (Barbados)

"By cablegram on Monday the eldest son of J G D'Aguiar learnt the sad tidings of his father's death in Barbados. Mr Jose Gomes D'Aguiar left these shores by the last mail for England where he purposed spending some time to recruit his health. The old gentleman who was one of the wealthiest of our citizens was wont to go to England for a change of air and scenery. On this occasion he was accompanied by his partner Mr Henrique Gomes de Faria. He leaves four sons to inherit the bulk of his fortune which is said to be about four hundred thousands dollars. ($400,000). One of the deceased's sons is a doctor who is now in England. The deceased was very much respected among his country men and citizens who knew him. He is said to have arrived in the colony from Madeira in the year 1842. He started a small provision business at Plantation M'ontrose and subsequently he traded at Plaisance. With that thrift and industry which characterize the Portuguese in this colony Mr D'Aguiar was not long in amassing a competence and at the time of his death he was possessed of two retail spirit shops and other household property in the city. He was also interested in eight retail spirit shops in various parts of the country.

(*The Daily Liberal,* 5 July, 1893)

Portuguese College

The annual distribution of prizes to the pupils of Portuguese College – 28th ult – Bishop Butler presiding. Previous to distribution, pupils went through a number of pieces in English and Portuguese in a very creditable manner and reflecting high credit on the ability, and zeal of the Principal, Mr E de M Brito Nobrega. Bishop congratulated Mr Nobrega – Portuguese parents should be thankful to have him in their midst –boys were very sharp – very intelligent. He was told by a gentleman-merchant in Water Street that boys educated at this College made better clerks than those educated in Madeira. Pupils all seemed very sharp in their Arithmetic – their minds active. "The great thing in education was to make the mind active". Bishop regretted school not larger, considering the number of Portuguese in city, he had expected number to be over 60 but it was not so. Portuguese not doing justice to themselves. "To bring up children in their language was best." "Whilst the English language was no doubt useful in this Colony in commercial life, yet a knowledge of his own language would (?) come more naturally to a Portuguese boy, than the English language, because it was his native tongue." Hoped the number would be increased next year. Those who were being educated under Mr Nobrega "would make intelligent young business men."

(*The Daily Chronicle* (Mail Edition) Wednesay 10 Jan 1894)

Portuguese Dramatic Performance

The Portuguese public in Georgetown were favoured with presentations of the drama in their native language on Wednesday evening in the Assembly Rooms, by some well known amateurs. The programme was divided into three parts opening with a drama in three acts "Scenes do Brazil," and comprising also the comedy "Choro on Rio", and the comedietta "Os dios Estroinas". The first was rather a trying piece for amateurs but the difficult characters were faithfully represented Messrs C De Freitas and J Silvano deserving special credit. The minor parts were also creditably represented by Miss Dos Santos, Messrs Ferreira and Fernandes. The comedy "Choro on Rio" was however the *pièce de resistance* of the evening's entertainment and deservedly so, not only on account of the piece itself but from the excellent presentation of it. The acting of Mr Fernandes, ably assisted by Miss Jardim and Mr Dias, was really of a high order, and repeatedly called for to the plaudits of the audience. In the last item on the programme the comedietta, the students were well represented by Messrs De Freitas and Ferreira each entering thoroughly into the spirit of his part. Mr Luiz Martins made a capable wealthy Brazilian, but was somewhat inclined to exaggerate his part. His acting however was highly praise worthy. Altogether the performance was very successful, and now that a start has been made there seems no reason why the Portuguese Dramatic Amateurs should not promote such highly enjoyable entertainments oftener. At the close of the evening the Rev Father Scoles and Barraud addressed the audience thanking them for their support, the proceeds being donated to the New Catholic College, Brickdam.

(*The Daily Chronicle,* Fri 4 May, 1894)

Recita Dramatica

Another Portuguese Dramatic Recital was given on Tuesday night under the patronage of Dr Des Nevas e Mello, the Portuguese Council, in the Assembly Rooms, where there was a fairly good attendance. The programme comprised three comedies of one act each, and a scene comica. The castes in the comedy consisted principally of those who appeared in the entertainment given some little time ago, and in some instances there was evidence of the actors having profited by the experience gained on that occasion. The first comedy entitled "Cada Doida" was very well staged, and in it C Dias showed to advantage as servant, while Luiz Martins and J A Santos, jnr as husband and wife, made a very creditable appearance. Mr F C Fernandes was warmly applauded, and deservedly so, for his humourous rendering of "Ananha vou Pedila". Mr Dias again took the part of the servant in the next comedy "Va ex Desculpe" and was again highly successful, thoroughly entering into the spirit of the part. The other characters were also very well represented. J Silvano as the dentist receiving perhaps the most applause. The last item on the programme was certainly not the least popular. "Laugh or Cry" is a bright little comedy and Costa Dias F C Fernandes, and Mr S C Fernandes who took the parts of the "go-between", husband and wife respectively, gave an excellent presentation of the idea of the author of the piece. The orchestra of twelve under the leadership of Mr J N N Noronha contributed largely to the success of the evening. After putting forward two such excellent entertainments as has been done by the promoters, it is a matter for rejust that they should have cause to complain that they do not receive that amount of support, which their endeavours certainly merit, and which is necessary to carry on successfully dramatic recitals.

(*The Daily Chronicle,* Thursday 7 June, 1894)

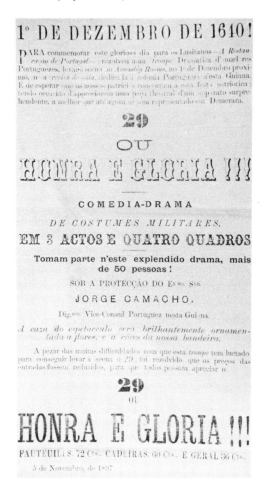

1st December of 1640

To commemorate this glorious day for the Portuguese – *The Restoration of Portugal* – ; a Dramatic *troup* of Portuguese amateurs has decided to stage in the *Assembly Rooms* on the 1st December next a *gala recital* dedicated to the Portuguese community in this Guiana. It is hoped that our countrymen will join in this patriotic celebration; taking this opportunity to appreciate a theatrical play of a remarkable production, the best that has yet been produced in Demerara.

29
OR
HONOUR AND GLORY!!!

Comedy-Drama
Of Military Costumes
In 3 Acts and Four Scenes
Taking part in this splendid
drama, more than 50 persons!

Under the patronage of His Excellency, Senhor Jorge Camacho,
Most worthy Portuguese Vice-Consul in Guiana.

The house of this spectacular will be brilliantly ornamented with
flowers and the colours of our flag.

In spite of the many difficulties with which this *troup* has struggled to stage this play of **29** it was decided to reduce the entrance fees in order that all will be able to appreciate.

29
OR
HONOUR AND GLORY!!!

Armchairs, 72 cts, Chairs, 60 cts and General Seats 36 cts.
5 of November 1897

(*Chronica Semenal,* 15 November 1897)

Centenary of Vasco da Gama – *Te Deum* Sung

The famous Portuguese navigator whose great discovery opened up the seaward route to the Indian Empire, though dead for four hundred of years, still lives in the memory of the Portuguese nation, in particular, and of all nations, in general. Reverence, gratitude, and admiration, all must be shared alike by Portuguese and British at calling to mind of that prowess and enterprise which brought honour to Lusitania, and wealth and power to Great Britain. Yesterday the cetenary of the great hero was celebrated by our Portuguese colonists throughout the land, and the jubilation of the moment was heartily participated in by British subjects. Owing to the necessity of calling a meeting of the Executive Council, His Excellency the Governor was unable to attend the Solemn *Te Deum* which was sung in the Church of the Sacred Heart, but this is no indication of any indifference in the event on the part of the British officials. The day was glorious with bright sunshine tempered by cooling breezes, and the streets presented a gay spectacle with the rich display of bunting and illuminated mottoes which ornamented several of the houses. The principal business premises of Portuguese merchants and store-keepers were the devices adopted for making the occasion one of gay and festivity. These are the occasions which keep alive the loyalty and faith of a people; loyalty to the country which calls them sons and daughters, faith in their own skill and enterprise as a nation. And it would be well if the centenary of Vasco de Gama and its cordial celebrations by colonists in general happily stirred some latent spark of loyalty in the hearts of all alike towards the country which gave many of us birth, and which affords all of us a living and a dwelling place – British Guiana, the *new and hopeful Colony* (mine). Let all colonists unite together in a strong endeavour to start industries which would promise to relieve *the present strain adversity,* and to encourage those obvious means of development which will bring to light the hidden wealth of Guiana; and even as we of this present generation now hail the name of da Gama with pride and great rejoicings, so a coming prosperity will celebrate with gladness the memory of those great deeds which shall be the first to lead to rearly as great discoveries on land as the gallant navigator made at sea. The difficulties may be as considerable, but the glory will be the same, while the benefits to our immediate descendants will be more substantial, and please God, for more permanent.

(*The Echo,* 16 July 1898)

4.º Centenario da descoberta do caminho para a India por VASCO DA GAMA

Uma *troupe* velocipidista de rapazes portuguezes, pensa tomar parte nos festejos que terão lugar n'esta cidade em honra do grande descobridor da India. Desde esse dia resolver-se-ha formar um club velocipidista "Vasco da Gama," sob a protecção do nosso representante de Portugal n'esta Guiana, o Ex.ᵐᵒ Sr. M. C. d'Almeida.

Todos os cyclistas devem apresentar-se no cortejo com as suas machinas ornamentadas a azul e branco. Para estimulo, resolveu-se crear 2 premios:—1.º "Vasco da Gama" $6.00; 2.º "Luiz de Camões" $4.00, para os dois que apresentem as suas bicycletas melhor enfeitadas.

Pede-se a todos os nossos patricios cyclistas que abrilhantem esta festa patriota.

O cortejo deve estar reunido as 4½ horas da tarde do dia 15 proximo, para partir ás 5. O sitio da partida é proximo ao Assembly Rooms.

Georgetown, 8 de Julho da 1898.

A COMMISSÃO.

Fourth Centenary of the Discovery of the
Sea Route to India by Vasco Da Gama

☆ ☆ ☆ ☆ ☆

A cycling *troupe* of Portuguese youth are desirous of taking part in our festivities which are to be celebrated in this city in honour of the great discoverer of India. From today they had decided to form a cycling club "Vasco da Gama" under the patronage of our representative of Portugal in Guiana his Excellency Senhor M C d'Almeida.

All cyclists should present themselves in procession with their machines decorated in blue and white.

As an incentive it has been decided to offer 2 prizes:- 1st "Vasco da Gama" $6.00 2nd "Luiz de Camões* $4.00, to those who will present themselves on the best decorated cycles.

Let us ask our patriotic cyclists to enhance this patriotic celebration.

The procession should form at 4.30 in the afternoon on the 15th next to start off at 5. The place of departure is next to the Assembly Rooms.

Georgetown, 8th July 1898.

The Committee

---

* Camões – Portuguese epic poet, greatest figure of Portuguese literature. Vasco da Gama's voyage is the main theme of this epic, *The Lusiads.*

(*Chronica Semanal,* 9 de Julho de 1898)

Vasco Da Gama Celebrations

Concert In the Promenade Gardens

A prominent feature of the celebrations in the afternoon was a concert in the Promenade Gardens at which the British Guiana Militia and the First of December Bands rendered selections. There was a large attendance as nearly all the Portuguese in business closed their premises and other employers gave the Portuguese members of their staff a holiday. In fact, the day was given up by a large majority of the Portuguese to festivities. Nearly all their houses or business premises were decorated with flags or bunting, and in some cases, such as the Ice House, the Kingston Chocolate Factory (both belonging to Messrs D'Aguiar Bros) the houses of Mr Jorge Comacho, Vice-Consul for Portugal, and Mr Abreu, of the firm of Messrs Rodrigues and Abreu, the decorations were tastefully arranged and elaborate. During the day nearly all the rum-shops, which bore signs of the national rejoicing, were closed. The Concert in the Gardens was most enjoyable and the selections rendered were well chosen, as will be seen from the programmes appended. The Consul for Portugal, Mr D'Almeida arrived about 3:15 o'clock, and he was received with the Portuguese National Anthem ("Hymna da Carta") played by the Militia Band. One of the most popular pieces on this Band's programme was the "Reminisences of all Nations," in which Mr Carroll, the Bandmaster, introduced the "Hymna da Carta." The popularity of this item was evidenced by the fact that notwithstanding the counter attraction of the Bicycle Parade passing the Gardens at the time it was played, a large number waited to hear it finished. The performance of the Primeiro de Dezembro Band also attracted a large audience.

Following are the programmes:-

Militia Band:- March, "Argandab"; Overture, "Village Festival" (O'Keefa); "Reminiscences of All Nations" (Arranged by Godfrey); Valse, "Mondnacht am Rhien" (Vallstedt); Fantaisie Espagnole, "Dolores" (Arranged by Hartman); Gavette, "Herzliebchen" (Bural); Valse, "Casino Tanze" (Gungl); Military Fantasia, "The Spanish Review" (Binding); Galop (Vocal) "Always Joyful" (Hecher).

THE CULTURAL CONTRIBUTION OF THE PORTUGUESE

First of December Band:- Portuguese National Anthem; March; "Lusitana"; Valse, Theresen; Overture, "Evening Thoughts"; Fantasia, "Songs of England"; Valse, "Waves of Danube"; Descriptive National Airs, "Alvadora Nacional"; Overture, "The Cross of Honour"; "Hymna da Carta"; "God Save the Queen."

Cyclists' Parade

During the afternoon a parade of cyclists on decorated "wheels" was held. The proposal originated outside of the celebration committee but when it was mooted to them it was readily received and as marking his appreciation of the suggestion the Portuguese Consul offered a prize of $10. Two other prizes were voted by the Committee. It was arranged that the parade should start in High Street opposite the Hand-in-Hand Buildings, at 4:30pm, but the crowd was so densely packed there that it was impossible to obtain a proper start notwithstanding the efforts of the Police. The cyclists, of whom thirty-three turned out, were accordingly directed to proceed to the Promenade Gardens and there a very good start was made. The route chosen was to the Botanic Gardens, where the cyclists were photographed, and back *via* Brickdam and High Street to the Promenade Gardens where the adjudications of the wheels took place. Mr M C D'Almeida, Portuguese Consul, chose the following as a committee to assist him in judging:- Mr Jorge Comacho, Dr D'Aguiar, Dr de Freitas, Messrs M Gomes, Julio Gonsalves, J Vieira and J B Francisco. They awarded the first prize to Messrs Isacc de Souza and J F Menezes who rode a tandem bicycle decorated to represent a ship named the "St Gabriel". The second prize was awarded to Mr F C Fernandes who rode a machine decorated like a ship, and in which he was "made up" to appear like Vasco da Gama as he appears in the various prints. Some difficulty was experienced in deciding the winner of the third prize, but it was finally awarded to Mr J F Vieira in consequence of his decorations being particularly appropriate to the occasion including as they did the Portuguese arms and a representative of Vasco da Gama. A special prize, subscribed for by the Judges was given to Jayme de

Nobrega, a young lad, for exceptionally tasteful way in which his bicycle was decorated. Another special prize was subscribed for by private persons and given to Mr Samuel Cozier he having a beautifully decorated wheel and being about the only black man who took part in the procession. The prizes will be distributed by the Portuguese Consul at a place and time which will be duly announced to the winners.

In the evening many of the dwelling houses of the Portuguese community were illuminated, and the buildings which deserved special mention were those marked by the excellence of the decorations during the day. The Ice House was a blaze of light with fairy lamps and Chinese lanterns, and on the western side the words "Vasco da Gama" were formed with a number of electric lights. The residences of Messrs Comacho and Abreu also attracted a lot of attention. Owing to the risk of fire there were no illuminations in Water Street, and as Mr D'Almeida could not consequently make any display at his office he co-operated with Mr Comacho in making a special display at the residence of the latter in Camp Street.

The Proceedings throughout were marked with complete success and reflected the great credit on the Committee which had charge of the arrangements and on the Portuguese Consul who presided over it. The celebrations will be concluded by a ball, the date of which will be announced when decided upon.

The Daily Chronicle, Sat 16th July, 1898

Vasco da Gama Cycling Club Formed

Mr M C D'Almeida, Portuguese Consul, on Friday night in the British Guiana Club distributed the prizes to the cyclists who were judged to have the best decorated wheels in the bicycle parade in connection with the Vasco da Gama celebrations on Friday, 15th instant. Names of the prize winners were: 1. Isaac de Souza and J F Menezes; 2. F C Fernandes; 3. Samuel Cozier.

At the close of the ceremony the meeting considered a proposal to form a Cycling Club confined to members of the Portuguese community, and it was unanimously decided that the "Vasco da Gama Cycling Club" should be formed. Over thirty members were enrolled and it is probable that the number will be largely increased.

(*The Daily Chronicle,* 24 July 1898)

[In British Guiana cycling became the rage. Macquarrie & Coy, Smith Bros, the Demerara Cycle Depot all advertised cycles. Articles appeared in the press re dangerous cycling and there were also Court cases for cyclists' claims for damages]

Proposed Portuguese String Band

A meeting was held the other evening at the residence of Mr A A Rodrigues, Barrack St, for the purpose of organising a new Portuguese String Band. Mr Rodrigues who presided, explained the object of the meeting, and after some discussion it was agreed that a new String Band should be started to be known as the "Academia de Amadores de Musica". It is to comprise three classes of numbers: performing members whose monthly subscription should be two shillings; performing members under tuition whose monthly subscription should be four shillings and non-performing members whose monthly subscription would be two shillings which would entitle them to admission at all public performances. The officers appointed were Messrs M C D'Almeida as President and Parton; A A Rodrigues, Vice-President; J De Freitas, Secretary; A R G Jasmims, Treasurer; and A H Fernandes and M R Gonçalves.

(*The Daily Chronicle,* Sunday, 7 August 1898)

Catholic School in Main Street

Opened on 1st September 1898
Everything related to business is taught.
Daily lessons in Portuguese
Terms:- $1.00 per month. Discount offered for Brothers of the Church.
The School is distinct from the others, and is well-ventilated and pleasant.

(*Chronica Semanal,* 3 September 1898)

Portuguese Boys' School

Children are enrolled for a moderate fee in this school attached to the Catholic Church in Main Street, where primary, elementary and intermediate instructions are taught – This is done every day from 9:00 am to 3:30 pm; and on Sundays from 10:00 to 11:00am.

Georgetown, October 1897

(*Chronica Semanal*, 25 December 1898)

Tuna União Recreativa Portugueza

"The Estudiantina Band"

A fairly numerous audience was attracted to the Assembly Rooms on Friday evening to hear the first concert given by the newly organised Estudiantina Band, consisting of about twenty young Portuguese citizens under the baton of Mr A Serrão. The whole performance was most enjoyable and was generally voted highly creditable to the band of young instrumentalists who have only been a few months in training. Mr Serrão himself deserves great praise for his untiring efforts, and on Friday evening he had the satisfaciton of conducting no less than five pieces of his own composition. The band consists largely of strings, the flute being the only reed instrument employed. Mandolins and braggas (a kind of small Portuguese guitar), supported by guitars, prevail and the 'cello combines very acceptably with the light instruments. With the exception of the duet for flute and cello all the items were well rendered, and the waltz "Dolores" was heartily encored. When the performers have had more practice they will learn to pay greater attention to light and shade and the braggas (*which were played by little boys*) will not show so marked a tendency to run away from the beat. The flautist also requires considerably more maturing before he is equal to duet or solo playing. Barring these few faults, the band acquitted itself with great credit and we look forward with pleasure to its future appearance before the public.

(*The Daily Chronicle*, Sunday, 9th October 1898)

Moonlight Concert – 22nd Anniversary of Primeiro de Dezembro Band

A concert of instrumental music was given at the Promenade Gardens on Wednesday night in commemoration of the restoration of Portugal and to celebrate the twenty-second anniversary of the Primeiro de Dezembro Band. The music was admirably selected and the programme was opened with the "Hymno da Carta constitutional of 1826" and the "Hymno de Restauração de Portugal" played by the Primeiro de Dezembro Band. The British Guiana Militia Band also played the Portuguese national tune before proceeding with other items for which it was put down on the programme, and the rendering was warmly received by the audience. Among the selections rendered by the Militia Band were some from Mascagni's *Cavalleria Rusticana,* a military formation by Bindus and (by desire) the Spanish Valse *Santiago* by Corbon. The Estudiantina String Band in their picturesque costumes proved to be a feature of the entertainment. They played some waltzes and marches in an extremely creditable manner and their efforts were deservedly applauded. The Primeiro de Dezembro Band, which promoted the concert, also played a number of selections which met with the appreciation of the audience. The attendance was fairly large, numbering between 500 and 600 people.

The Daily Chronicle, Friday 2nd Dec 1898)

Portuguese Mayor of Georgetown – elected 3 Jan 1899

Elected town Councilor – November 1898 – for Charlestown ward Manoel Loexetto Da Costa – born in the Island of Madeira in 1862 and came to this colony with his parents in 1869. He first went into Water Street as cashier in the store of Mr Tom Gilbert in 1874; in 1876 he entered the employ of "Weston's" (afterwards Da Silva and Gouveia); and in 1878 he was taken on at Mr D H McGowan's. In 1882 he was admitted into partnership with Mr McGowan in the Cart Market store; but a few years later he severed his connection with the firm and started the Bazaar Store, in partnership with the late Mr M Gonsalves, under the name, style and firm of Gonsalves, Costa and c. In 1887 he was again admitted into partnership with Mr D H McGowan and has continued since then as the resident partner in the business known as the Grand Central, which is admitted to be one of the foremost dry goods businesses in this city. He was first elected as Town Councillor in 1894 and is now on his third term of service. He is chairman of the Portuguese Pawn Brokery Company, a Director of the British Guiana Rice Company, and was a Director of the Lusitania Ice Company, and of the Rental Purchase Society. In October 1896 he became a naturalized British Subject, and in March 1898, he was appointed the Portuguese representative on the Commission to enquire into the system of levying the duty on rum sold by retail spirit dealers, but he left the colony on furlough before the Commissioners' labours were brought to a close. He is a member of the Demerara Club, and had been connected with many other social institutions in the Colony.

(*The Echo,* 7 Jan 1899)

Professions

Intelligence has been received that Mr Cesar Augusto de Faria, eldest son of Mr Augusto Cesar de Faria of this City has passed his final course of Examinaiton as Doctor in medicine, etc at the Paris University. He proceeds to England to obtain an English diploma to enable him to practise his profession in this Colony.

(*The Daily Chronicle,* 20 August, 1898)

Amongst the names of those presented for the degree of Doctor of Medicine at Edinburgh University on July 30 we find that of Casmiro Joaquim Gomes of Demerara, MB,CM (1891). Dr Gomes is known to a large circle of friends in this Colony, and the news of his success will be received with pleasure.

(*The Daily Chronicle,* 26 August, 1898)

Portuguese Celebrate Emancipation Day as a Holy Day
HOLY DAY

Monday of this week was declared a holy day it being the anniversary of the emancipation of the slaves.

Horse-races were held at the hippodrome of our compatriot, his Excellency Luis Fernandes, in the beautiful village of Victoria, where the crowd from the city reached nearly 3,000.

There was a steamboat excursion to *Sand Hill,* where the excursionists had a good time, and there was also a concert on board the steamboat.

(Chronica Semanal, 12 August 1899)

J P Santos' Wedding
Wedding at Brickdam Cathedral
Santos – Mendonca

A large congregation assembled in the Brickdam Catheral, yesterday afternoon, to witness the nuptials of Mr J P Santos, head of the well known firm of J P Santos & Co, and Miss Marie Jose Mendonca, second daughter of Mr Manoel Mendonca, jnr. The interior of the Cathedral had undergone some slight floral decoration, a bridal arch being erected at the entrance to the sanctuary, and lots of maiden hair fern being grouped on either side of the sanctuary steps. Mr A de Weever precided at the organ, and played several appropriate selections of music pending the arrival of the bridal party. The bride entered the Cathedral with her father, by whom she was given away – to the strains of Gounod's "Wedding March", the "Promenade Militaire" by Naumann being played on the arrival of the bridegroom. The bride's costume was of Oriental Satin trimmed with Brussels lace and white silk applique embroidered tulle veil, and handsome Court train, set off at the end by a lover's knot of orange blossom. The bride who wore a diamond crescent and diamond bracelets, the gift of the bridegroom, carried a shower bouquet of eucharis lilies, stephanotis, and maiden hair fern. She was attended by four bridesmaids – the Misses Mendonca (sister) Gonsalves, De Abreu and Nascimento (cousins). These young ladies looked well in white crêpe de chine trimmed with ecru appliqué and hats of green silk, adorned with black velvet and pink roses. Their ornaments, provided by the bridegroom, consisted of gold bangles. They also carried shower bouquets of pink and white roses and maiden hair fern. Mr J S Gonsalves officiated as best man. Many handsome costumes were worn by the ladies of the wedding party. Mrs Mendonca, mother of the bride, chose velvet voile, trimmed with ecru insertion and a black hat set off with ecru lace and pink roses.

Mrs M J de Freitas wore black net with lovers' knots, with black hat to match. Mrs Gonsalves had on helitrope foulard trimmed with cream lace insertion, and a black hat with violet flowers. A pretty costume was that of Mrs M Perreira – cream voile over pink glace silk, with hat to match. Mrs Comacho wore grey silk, trimmed with white appliqué and white satin frills and a chiffon hat of marguerites. Mrs D M Huston attended in eau de nil and black and white hat. Mrs J A Ferreira chose a lovely gown of grey voile. Mrs Charles Gonsalves had on grass ecru silk over violet silk and ecru appliqués and black chiffon hat. Miss Baptista appeared in white organdie muslim trimmed with lace, and black hat. After the ceremony, which was performed by Bishop Galton, assisted by Fathers Sidgreaves and Gambetti, Wagner's Bridal March was played during the signing of the register, followed by Mendelssohn's Wedding March as the party left the Cathedral.

A reception was afterwards held at the residence of the bride's parents in Middle Street. Among those invited, or who were present were: Dr and Mrs de Freitas, Mr and Mrs G J de Freitas, Dr and Mrs Jardim, Mr and Mrs Rodrigues, Mrs M J de Freitas, Miss Pereira, Mr, Mrs and Misses D'Andrade, Mr and Mrs M Nascimento, Miss Rodrigues, Mrs and Miss Nascimento, Mr and Mrs F Mathias, Mr and Mrs J C Fernandes, Mrs Augusta D'Abreu, Mr, Mrs and Miss da Silva, Mr J C Paira, Mr, Mrs and Miss Soares, Mr and Mrs J Walls, Mrs Eliza and Miss Mendonca, Mrs da Costa, Mr M J Texeira, Mr Q D'Abreau, Mr and Mrs and Misses Mendonca, Mrs D Gomes and Misses Gomes, Mr and Mrs J Henriques, Bishop Galton, Fathers Gambetti, Victorine, Justino, Pollen, Darby, McCormick, Gillet, Cassati, Brother Reynolds, Mr J and Miss Henriques, Mr J Henriques jnr, Mrs Gonsalves, Mr E Gonsalves, Mr J Gonsalves, Mrs and Misses Gonsalves, Mr M Mendonca, Miss D'Andrade, Mr Narcisco D'Andrade, Mr Castellani, Mr, Mrs and Miss Pereira, Mr and Mrs J Comacho, Mr and Mrs Carlos Gonsalves, Mr and Mrs J Dias, Mr and Mrs and Miss Garraway, Mr and Mrs M P Comacho, Mr and Mrs Jasmins, Mr and Mrs J Fereira, Mr and Mrs M Gomes, Mr and Mrs Ferreira, Mr and Mrs M Faria, Mr and Mrs J Faria, Mr and Mrs A Gomes,

Mr Vieira, Mr and Mrs J G Rodrigues, Mr, Mrs and Miss de Freitas, Mrs and Miss Gaskin, Mr, Mrs and Miss Fernandes, Mr, Mrs and Misses Capello, Mr and Misses Welchman, Mrs Pereira, Mrs and Misses Melville, Mr and Mrs Ridley, Mr Benson, Mr B S Conrad, Mr and Mrs Abrams, Miss Gonsalves, Mr and Mrs D Gomes, Mr, Mrs and Misses Mendonca, Mr, Mrs and Miss Dargan, Mr Stokes and Father Purcell.

Mr and Mrs J P Santos subsequently left for Blankenburg, where the honeymoon is being spent. The bride's travelling dress being of cream muslim over blue, with black velvet ribbon, and white hat with pink roses.

(*The Daily Chronicle*, Friday, 3 October 1902)

Death of Mr M L R Andrade
Highly Respected Colonist

Sad Event In Paramaribo Hospital

News reached the colony by telegram on Sunday of the death in Paramaribo of Mr M L R Andrade, at the Roman Catholic Hospital at 3:40pm that day.

Mr Andrade left the colony for Paramaribo with his daughter Mrs T F Kevin-Green on the 7th February last and underwent an operation at the Hospital on Wednesday last. The operation was reported successful; but the patient developed pneumonia and despite all efforts to save him, died on Sunday as stated above. He was 71 years of age.

Mr Andrade who was one of the best known and most respected Portuguese gentlemen in the colony, was born in Madeira and received his early education at Mount St Mary's College, England. He then entered a military school in Lisbon and was still quite young when the Carlist War broke out in Spain. He at once joined the Carlist army and served throughout the campaign, the end five years later finding him with the rank of Captain.

In 1882 he came to the Colony to claim some money left him as a minor in the care of the administrator General. He remained in the colony and obtained employment with a few firms including that of Messrs George Little & Co, and Wieting & Richter.

In 1885 he went to Venezuela where he married the Senorita Anita Nunea, a wealthy Spanish lady. He then returned to the colony and launched out in the cattle business. During 1887-89 he was Venezuelan Consul and had much to do with the settling of the boundary question between British Guiana and Venezuela. The cattle business had however proved a failure; and in 1894 he started the old Demerara Ice House then known as the Lusitania Ice Co. He subsequently went to Panama as representative of the Swift Packing Co, and established branches of this firm in Panama and Colon. He returned to the colony in 1910 and was appointed auditor of Messrs J P Santos & Co, Ltd, at its inception. He was also auditor of the B G Biscuit Factory Ltd, Messrs Lopes & Co Ltd, and C De Abreu Ltd, (from their inception), G Bettencourt & Co, Ltd, and the B G and Trinidad Fire Insurance Co Ltd, while he was also Secretary of the Guiana Match Factory Co Ltd, a director of the Portuguese Pawnbroking Co, Ltd, one of the Appraisers of the Mayor and Town Council and Vice Consul for Portugal.

Mr Andrade besides being a man of exceptional business talent, spoke fluently English, Spanish, Portuguese, French and Italian. He leaves a widow, one son – Mr Herman Andrade, manager of the Guiana Match Factory, two daughters – Mesdames F P Camacho and T F Kevin-Green, five grandsons and one grand-daughter to mourn their loss.

Chairmen of British Guiana's Local Authorities
Biographical Sketches. No 33 of a Series
Mr Manoel de Aguiar of Meadow Bank

Mr Manoel De Aguiar, more popularly known as 'Mannie' de Aguiar has been honoured by the Local Government Board for the past twenty years by being appointed a Councillor for the Meadow Bank Country District, but since February 1, 1938, the highest honour of Chairman Vice Hon J I de Aguiar, on leave, was conferred on him.

Mr de Aguiar, who is a cousin of the Hon J I de Aguiar, was born on March 3rd 1897 to Caroline, wife of Mr Manoel de Aguiar.

His education was placed in the capable hands of Mr T W A Dathorne, of the now defunct Meadow Bank RC School.

Leaving school at an early age, young de Aguiar spent three years at the Stewartville Spirit Shop, West Coast Demerara, where he began to learn the delicate art of blending rums. But rural business life seemed to have held no charms for him and he emigrated to the city, once more taking up residence at Meadow Bank.

Mr de Aguiar quickly secured employment at Messrs Santos de Caires and Co, now defunct, and after three years' service there, he joined the firm of Messrs G Bettencourt and Co Ltd. In 1924, Mr de Aguiar again changed his working connexions and from the date he has been with Messrs J P Santos and Co Ltd. From a junior clerk, after 14 years' service he has risen to the post of Receiving Customs Clerk.

Mr de Aguiar is held in popular esteem by his fellow-clerks. He takes a keen interest in cricket and is a lover of the game, being one of the founders of the Meadow Bank Cricket Club, and is still its president.

He is one of those who were instrumental in getting the Hon C R Jacob to present a cup for competition on the East and West Bank, Demerara. A devoted Roman Catholic, Mr de Aguiar has been Sacristan for the Meadow Bank Roman Catholic Church for 22 years.

Asked which he considered to be the biggest single step on the road of progress that his village had made during his twenty years as a member of the Council, Mr de Aguiar promptly averred that the erection of a huge concrete cistern to store rain water undoubtedly stood out clearly above everything. He believed that Meadow Bank was the only village throughout British Guiana that had a rainwater storage system that could supply its villagers with water in time of drought. The water is supplied freely to villagers.

Mr de Aguiar married Miss Mary Gomes, daughter of the late Antonio Gomes and Mrs Ludwina Gomes of D'Urban Street.

His children – 3 boys and 2 girls – form the central part of his life. They were born at Meadow Bank. Mr de Aguiar himself was born at Meadow Bank.

(*Daily Chronicle* Sunday 3 July, 1938)

Obit of G J de Freitas
British Guiana Mourns Passing of Mr G J de Freitas

Leader of the Bar dies in England
(Daily Chronicle Special Correspondent.) Georgetown. Tuesday July 12, 1938

The "Daily Chronicle" announces with profound regret the end of a great career. MR GUILHERME JOSE DE FREITAS, K C, died yesterday morning before 9 o'clock (British Guiana time) at Waltham-on-Thames, London. His death had for some time been daily expected, but the end will none the less be a deep shock, for in him British Guiana has lost a man who illustrates fully the perfect Guianese Gentleman. Mr de Freitas was ailing for some time. Towards the end of last year he went to London for treatment during which time he underwent a major operation for the amputation of one of his legs. He was suffering from a dangerous malady from which he never recovered, despite the best medical skill and attention England could offer.

About two months ago he was strong enough to join a pilgrimage to Lourdes in France. He returned to England in mid-June. With him in England at the time of his death were his devoted wife, his elder brother, Dr J M de Freitas and Mrs de Freitas, and his younger sister, Mrs F E Cherry. His sister-in-law, Mrs Raleigh left British Guiana a few days ago hoping to reach his bedside. The news of his death reached her in Trinidad this morning. She is proceeding on her journey.

OBSEQUIES IN ENGLAND
The obsequies will take place in England tomorrow. In Georgetown there will be a Solemn Requiem at the Brickdam Cathedral of the Immaculate Conception tomorrow morning at 7 o'clock.

Shortly after the receipt of the cable announcing his death, the city went into mourning. The Chambers of Messrs Cameron and Shepherd, Solicitors, the legal firm of which Mr de Freitas was one of the principals, and the business of Messrs de Souza and Mendonca, Lombard Street, was closed, while the flags at the Portuguese Consulate, the Town Hall, the Banks, the many business houses in Water Street and about, and the principal Sporting Clubs were lowered to half mast.

In the Supreme Court, the Acting Chief Justice, the Puisne Judge, and members of the two branches of the legal profession met and paid tribute to his memory. A report of the proceedings appears on p7.

Mr de Freitas has left to mourn his death, his widow, two brothers, Dr J M de Freitas and Mr Stanley de Freitas (Lisbon) and six sisters, Mesdames F A Francis (USA), F E Cherry (London), J A M Pacheco, P M d'Aguiar, and M J Rodrigues, and Miss Lily de Freitas. To these and his many other relatives the "Daily Chronicle" begs to offer its profound sympathy.

(*Daily Chronicle* Tuesday 12 July, 1938)

"Portugal Was Proud of Him"

(By Senhor Manoel Fernandes, Consul for Portugal in British Guiana)

The death of Mr G J de Freitas removes from this community one who has been the embodiment of the true gentleman of Portugal. British subject to birth, Portugal was proud of him, none the less. Loyal and devoted to his King and Country, he was at heart a Portuguese, and during his life time did everything in his power to uphold the proud traditions of the race. He was the legal adviser to the Consulate in British Guiana, and we shall miss him greatly.

Like the rest of the community, the Portuguese here have lost a real friend. He took a keen interest in everything that tended to promote the best interests of his parent's country. He was conversant with the arts, the sciences, and the literature of the nation, and he was interested in its laws and developments as those of England. He was an honour to his race, as he was to British Guiana, and the British Empire as a whole.

(*The Daily Chronicle* Wednesday, 20 July 1938)

Portuguese Scholars

Mr Percy De Caires, Guiana Scholar, 1932 graduated from Edinburgh University with degrees MB, CL.B.

Dr De Caires was the first student to win the Scholarship from St Stanislaus College and studied Science at QC for one year prior to entering Edinburgh in 1933.

(*Missionary Magazine,* Vol 2. No 16, Oct 1938, p190)

RIP (1935) Death of G J De Freitas, KC – most brilliant of the practising member of the bar. "He was also the most capable and consistent in his general deportment and character. (Mr J T Clark) (J A Veersaswamy, Presiding Magistrate) – . . . "while Mr de Freitas was possessed of keen intellect and applied himself to his duties the success he attained was due to the fact that he was a deeply religious man whose life was an example not only to fellow practitioners, but to all citizens."

(*Missionary Magazine*, Vol 2. No. 16, Oct 1938, p191)

Chairmen of British Guiana's Local Authorities
Biographical Sketches. No 35

HUIS T'DIEREN COUNTRY DISTRICT
MR V G MENEZES

Mr Vincent Gonsalves Menezes is Chairman of the Huis T'Dieren Country District, and has held this post for the past eleven years. Prior to that he was a councillor for five years.

He was born at Prazeres in the lovely island of Madeira on December 24, 1893, to Mr Ignatius Gonsalves Menezes and his wife Marcia, née Rodrigues. Arriving in British Guiana at the age of 13, young Menezes without being able to read or write started to work with the late Mr A F Cabral in the City. He was afterwards employed with Mr Dos Santos at the Botanic View Spirit Shop.

Being ambitious and thirsting for knowledge, young Vincent started to take private tuition with Mr J M Cox with the object of fitting himself for the years that lay ahead of him.

In 1913, Mr Menezes arrived on the Essequibo Coast, and he has remained there from that day to now. After starting on the Coast with Mr A J Da Silva he branched out on his own in the provision and dry goods business in 1919. In the same year, he went into partnership in a rice milling business but this partnership was dissolved in 1925.

Mr Menezes was also extensively interested in the wood cutting industry and at one time was a contractor to the then Colonial Transport Department. He is a radio enthusiast and years ago, before radio was popularized, he successfully experimented in building up radio sets.

Today, his is the only radio service from Supenaam to Charity and his services are frequently sought for attending "sick radios."

For some months now, Mr Menezes has entered the theatre business in partnership with his brother-in-law, Mr M I Jardim, and they own the new and attractively built "Atlantis Cinema" at Suddie.

He was married in 1917 to Mary Jardim by which union there has been a child.

His principal hobby is the radio and motor-car driving. He was appointed a councillor in 1922 and Chairman since 1927.

For years now he has been agitating for a pure water supply and irrigation for the rice farming section of the District by tapping the Iteribisci. His scheme was accepted years ago by the Government, who sent up surveyors and Engineers, but since then, the matter has been lying dormant. Recently, however, the village has been given well-water piped 4½ miles away at Onderneeming.

In higher politics, Mr Menezes identifies himself with all electioneering campaigns and his opposition to anyone's candidature is much dreaded.

(*Daily Chronicle*, Sunday 31 July, 1938)

Customs

Feast of the Holy Spirit or Pentecost. May or June

During the nine days previous to the Feast of the Holy Spirit, the *Emperador* visited all the Catholic homes of the poor and the sick in his parish/village carrying with him a dove and a crown into which the people placed their money-gift to be used in celebration of the Feast. After the Mass of the Feast a dinner was usually held for the poor and clothing distributed.

Feast of St John The Baptist. 24th June

This was a favourite feast especially among the young Portuguese. Bonfires were lit and the young men competed with each other in seeing who could jump the highest. Another custom on this feast was the breaking of eggs into a basin of water; whatever shape the egg formed would determine the person's fate, viz., a ship meant travel.

Feast of St Peter. 29th June

This feast was dear to the fishermen and celebrated particularly between Meadowbank and La Penitence. The fishermen carried a boat (lifeboat size) in procession singing and waving flags. St Peter is the patron saint of fishermen and very special beloved by Madeirans many of whom earned their livelihood by fishing.

Feast of St Anthony – 13th June

The saint, par excellence of Portuguese devotions both in Portugal and Madeira and transferred to Guyana was Saint Anthony. The custom of St Anthony's Bread has been of long duration in this country. On this day of his feast, 13th June, bread loaves topped with a cross are distributed to the poor and needy.

Feast of All Souls – 2nd November

Another custom brought from Madeira was the lighting of candles on the graves of loved ones on All Souls night.

Christmas Novena – 15th-23rd December

The Madeiran custom of attending Mass in the early hours of the morning, viz. 5:30am (in the 19th century the churches opened at 4:30am) for the nine days preceding Christmas continues to this day in Guyana. People of every ethnic group, and many not even of Catholic faith, participate in this service and together before Mass they sing praises to the Mother of God in the *Bemdita Sejaes*. The Mass concludes with the Benediction of the Blessed Sacrament.

Christmas Mass

After the Shepherd's Mass or the Second Mass of Christmas Day at Sacred Heart Church, Main Street, children dressed in Portuguese costume brought various gifts of food: large loaves of bread, chickens, a lamb, etc. to offer them to the Infant Jesus in the crib. These gifts were given afterwards to the needy.

Bemdita Sejaes

Salve, o doce amparo
Dos tristes mortaes,
Virgem sempre pura,
Bemdita sejaes.

Bemdita sejaes!
Bemdita sejaes!
Nos ceus e na terra
Bemdita sejaes.

Salve, Rainha!
Que Mae vos chamaes
De Misericordia!
Bemdita sejaes.

Sois vida e decora
Dos filhos que amaes,
Esperanca nossa;
Bemdita sejaes.

Salve, a vos bradamos;
Ouvi nossos ais,
Que a vos se dirigem!
Bemdita sejaes.

Lembrae – vos de nos,
Pos em perigos taes
Somos degredados;
Bemdita sejaes.

Os Filhos de Eva
Os afflictos mortaes,
Por vos suspiramos
Bemdita sejaes.

Gemendo e chorando
Vos nos consolaes
em nosso desterro;
Bemdita sejaes.

N'este valle lagrimas,
De penas fataes,
Sempre vos cantamos;
Bemdita sejaes.

Eia, o Mae benigna,
Que nos illustraes;
Por tudo Senhora,
Bemdita sejaes.

Advogada Nossa,
Tanto vos dignaes,
De rogar por todos, . . .

Esses vossos olhos
Que não tem oguaes
Ponde em nos Senhora; . . .

Misericordiosos,
Como costumaes
Anos os volvei; . . .

E depois de acabar
Fadigas penaes
Do nosso desterro; . . .

Nos Mostrae a Jesus
Na gloria aonde estaes
Para sempre o Louvar; . . .

O bemdito fructo,
Que nos offertaes
Para o possuirmos; . . .

Monstrae-nos os dons
Que vos nos guardaes
Bens do vosso ventre; . . .

Que nunca o percamos
Nao o permittaes;
O Virgem clemente, . . .

O Mae piedosa,
Que nos abrigaes;
O doce Maria, . . .

Sempre, Virgem bella,
Louvores geraes
Vos deem ceos a terra; . . .

Bemdita, e bemdita
Mil vezes, e mais,
O Virgem Maria, . . .

Rogae vos por nos;
Não vos esquecaes;
Santa Mae de Deus . . .

Para sermos dignos,
Em instantes finaes,
De cantarmos sempre; . . .

Das promessas de Christo
Vos nos seguraes;
Soberana Rainha, . . .

Assim seja sempre,
Sempre, e muito mais,
Amen Jesus;
Bemdita sejaes.

Portuguese Foods

1. Bolo do mel (molasses cake)

2. Bacelhau (saltfish)

3. Carne do alho (garlic pork)

4. Malassados (lightly-cooked)/sonhos (dreams)
   (pancakes made on Shrove Tuesday – Pancake day)

5. Cus-cus

6. Cabbage and pumpkin soup

7. Red bean soup (sopa de feijão)

8. Garlic soup with egg

9. Pumpkin fritters

10. Beef stew with plaited bread

11. Espetada

12. Madeira Wines

13. Milho (corn meal)

14. Broas (biscuits)

Glossary of some Portuguese Words in use in Guyana

avo	grandmother
alpargatas	leather soled slippers worn by Portuguese shopmen
arroz	rice
bacelhau	salt fish
bolo de mel	molasses cake
briga	pugnacious (from 'brigar' = to fight)
cabeza no tem juizo	you're crazy!
cala boca	keep quiet!
caviche	fish, soaked in vinegar with onions, garlic, thyme, hot peppers.
Josie	name for Portuguese shopkeeper
Mannie	another name for Portuguese shopkeeper
manniezing	Portuguese shop assistant
mas fica	more remains
olhado	bad eye
si deus quizer	God willing!
Quandos porcos balu, vem shuva	when the pigs dance, rain will fall (when one is too gay, trouble will come)

Mr Peter d'Aguiar, former Minister of Finance and leader of the United Force, Proprietor of Banks, DIH, receiving The Peace Medal, USA

Past and Present Prominent Portuguese in Business, Politics, Professions and Sport

BUSINESS

Basil Andrade (Director, J P Santos & Co Ltd)
Hernan Jorge Andrade (Manager, Guyana Match Factory)
Marcelle Andrade (Travel Agent, Frandec)
Clement Bettencourt-Gomes, BEM (Managing Director, G Bettencourt & Co Ltd)
Frank Brazão (Commission Agent)
Theerese Brazao (Orinduik)
Frederick Pereira Camacho (Director, M P Camacho, Ltd)
George Camacho (Chairman, Guyana & Trinidad Mutual Fire Insurance Co Ltd)
Olive Correia (Proprietor and Director, Correia's Jewellery Establishment)
E F Correia (Diamond Merchant)
Euguene Correia (Manager, Correia's Esso Service Station)
Hilary Correia (Owner & Manager, Astor Cinema)
M C Correia (Diamond Trader)
Mike & Stephen Correia (Proprietors, Correia's Enterprises Ltd)
John Ignatius D'Aguiar (Managing Director, J P Santos & Co, Ltd)
Peter Stanislaus D'Aguiar (Managing Director, Banks Breweries, Ltd)
Henry D'Andrade (Manager, Bookers Bros, Bartica)
Manoel ('Kruger') D'Andrade (Proprietor, M D'Andrade Paint Co, Ltd)
A B De Caires (Director, De Caires Bros)
Cecil De Caires (Managing Director, Frandec Travel Service)
Francis De Caires (Commission Agent and Manufacturers' Representative)
Francis Ignatius De Caires (Director, De Caires Bros, Ltd)
Salvador De Caires (Governing Director, De Caires Bros, Ltd)
Jules Harold De Cambra, A A (Director, New Building Society)
Flavio Da Silva (Gold and Diamond miner and trader)
Gaston Da Silva (Proprietor & Manager Polar Bear Bar)
Manoel Ferreira Da Silva (Sawmill Proprietor and Operator)
Antonio De Castro (Wine Manufacturer & Proprietor, De Castro's Wine Factory)
Arlindo, Decio, Roger and Sergius De Freitas (Directors, Charlestown Saw Mills)
Celestino De Freitas (Managing Director, Central Garage)

Mr Eric Rodrigues
Manager
Royal Bank of Canada
Georgetown, 1958-1967

Dr J A Gomes, MBE, Proprietor of Schuler & Gomers 1932-1974

BUSINESS (contd)

John De Freitas (Central Garage: Proprietor)
John Simon De Freitas (Present Managing Director, Central Garage)
Silvestro Simão De Freitas, (Governing Director, Charlestown Sawmills)
Henry De Lima (Manager & Proprietor, De Lima's Leather Store)
Roy De Mattos (Secretary, Portuguese Pawnbroking Co, Ltd)
Alvaro Joseph De Souza (Manager, Bookers Motor Dept)
João Baptista De Souza (confectioner)
Antonio Calisto Gonsalves Dos Santos (Manager, Virtue & Co)
B A Fernandes, A A (Managing Director, John Fernandes, Ltd)
Billy Fernandes (Bounty Farm)
Christoopher Fernandes (Secretary, John Fernandes Ltd)
John Fernandes, OBE (Shipping & Commission Agent)
Carlos Fernandes (Manager, B G Biscuit Factory)
Stanley Fernandes (Manager, D M Fernandes, Ltd)
Victor Fernandes (Manager, Fogarty's Philharmonic Hall)
C P Ferreira (Director, F G Ferreira, Ltd)
Alvaro Druce Gomes, MBE (Chairman, Ferreira & Gomes, Ltd)
Victor Gomes (Commission Agent)
Clement Gonsalves (Director, M Gonsalves, Ltd)
Edward M Gonsalves (Director, Charlestown Saw Mills, Ltd)
Helena Gonsalves (Proprietor, Park Hotel)
Julio Bernardine Gonsalves (Manager, Fogarty's Wholesale Store)
Noel Gonsalves, A A (Managing Director, J P Santos & Co Ltd)
John Jardim (Managing Director, J P Santos & Co Ltd)
Jorge Jardim (Manager, Singer Sewing Machine Co)
A J Lopes (Managing Director, Lopes Bedstead & Furniture Co)
George Lopes (Proprietor, Standard Pawnbrokery Ltd)
R S Lopes (Proprietor, Alec Russell & Co)
Stanislaus Ignatius Martins (Branch Manager, Manufacturers' Life Insurance Co)
Derek & June Mendes (Proprietors, Farfan & Mendes)
Frank Mendonca (Chairman, M de Mendonca & Co, Ltd)
José Mendonca (Spirit Shop Proprietor and Rum Blender)
Vincent Gonsalves Menezes MBE (Timber Dealer, Essequibo)
John Rodrigues Nascimento (Manager, Pawnbroker and Partner, Central Pawnbrokery)
Joseph Nunes (Director, Wm Fogarty Ltd & Briana Manufacturing Co, Ltd)
J N Perreira (Merchant)
Cecil and Cyril Perreira (Directors, Brown Betty Dairies Ltd)
V Pires (Chairman, B G Canning Co)
Augustus (Narvo) Pestano (Managing Director, Pestano Outfit Store)
Clifford Barrington Reis (Proprietor of Aerated Water Factory)
Ignatius Gonsalves Rebeiro, J P (Estate Proprietor & Rice and Cattle Farmer)
Lionel Rodrigues (Director, Rodrigues & Rodrigues, Ltd)
J P Santos (Founder, J P Santos & Co Ltd)
John M Teixeira (Manager, International Pawnbrokery)

THE HONOURABLE FRANCIS DIAS, OBE

The First Portuguese in the Executive Council, also
Mayor of Georgetown and the first Portuguese
to receive the OBE

POLITICS
John Caldeira
Hon Eugene Francis Correia, MP
Hon J I D'Aguiar, MLC
Peter S D'Aguiar (Former leader of the United Force Party)
Manoel D'Aguiar (Chairman, Meadowbank Country District)
Eleanor Da Silva, MP
Hon Francis Dias, OBE (Mayor of Georgetown)
Hon John Fernandes, OBE
Hon Clement Patrick Ferreira, MLC, Mayor of New Amsterdam
Hon E M Gonsalves (Mayor of Georgetown)
Hon Mrs Helga Gonsalves (Mayoress of Georgetown)
Hon Joseph Gonsalves, OBE (Mayor of Georgetown)
Ann Jardim (Ambassador to Venezuala)
John Gabriel Joaquim, JP, OBE
V G Menezes (Chairman, Huis T'Dieren Country District)
Christopher Nascimento, MP
Joseph Gomes Pimento

PROFESSIONS
Stan J R Affonso, A A (Managing Director, Royal Bank of Canada/National Bank of Industry and Commerce)
A M S Barcellos
John Barcellos (accountant)
Dr Silvio Bettencourt-Gomes, OBE
A C and Iris Brazão (lawyers)
A F Camacho (Steward, Public Hospital)
Frank D'Abreu (Inspector of Police)
W P D'Andrade, CMG (First Guyanese Governor, Bank of Guyana)
Clement Da Silva (accountant)
David De Caires (lawyer)
Dr Percy De Caires
Caesar P De Freitas (surveyor)
G J De Freitas (Leader of the Bar)
Herman W De Freitas (lawyer)
J Edward De Freitas (lawyer)
Dr Q B De Freitas
S S De Freitas (Consul for Portugal)
A J De Souza (lawyer)
Bernard Dos Santos (lawyer)
Francis Ignatius Dias (solicitor)
Dr Norbert Dias (GMO, Public Hospital)
Vivian Charles Dias (solicitor)
Sr M Gabriel Fernandes, RSM (Principal, St Joseph High School)
Manoel Fernandes (Vice-Consul for Portugal)
Joseph Passion Ferreira (professional photographer)
Carlos Gomes, OBE (lawyer)

Mrs Vera Lopes, donor of the Lopes Challenge Cup for Ladies Inter-Club Table Tennis and one of the best women players in the Colony.

Mr Willie Matthias and Mrs Muriel Delgado, Champion Tennis Players

PROFESSIONS (contd)

Dr J A Gomes, MBE (optometrist)
Sir Stanley Gomes (Chief Justice)
Olga Gomes, LRSM (musician)
W I Gomes (editor)
Ulric Gouveia (broadcaster)
Dr D K Jardine (CMO, Mackenzie Hospital)
Sr Therese Marie Marques, RSM (Principal, St Joseph High School) (Administrator, St Joseph Mercy Hospital)
Sr M Noel Menezes, RSM, AA (Professor of History, University of Guyana)
Jayme Augusto Machado Pacheco (Clerk of Markets, Georgetown)
Michael Pereira, LRSM (organist)
Albert Rodrigues (architect)
Eric Rodrigues (Manager, Royal Bank of Canada)
Dr Charles Roza, OBE (CMO, Mackenzie Hospital)
Olga Lopes Seale, MBE (broadcaster)

GUYANA SCHOLARS

Percy De Caires
Joceyln D'Oliveira
Anne Jardim
Albert Ferraz

SPORT

Bridge

John Simon De Freitas
Romeo Delgado
Victor Lopes

Cricket

George Camacho, Jnr
Stephen Camacho
Jules Chabrol
Cecil De Caires
Frank De Caires
Arlindo De Freitas
Celso De Freitas
Roger De Freitas
Sergius De Freitas
M P Fernandes
Oscar Wright, MBE

Croquet

P S D'Aguiar

Cycling

Fred Baptista
Desmond De Caires
David De Freitas
Ian D'Ornellas
Herman Gomes

Football and Rugby

Louis Da Silva
Mannie Da Silva
Murphy Da Silva
Arlindo De Freitas
Celso De Freitas
Roger De Freitas
Sergius De Freitas
Bobby Fernandes
Carlos Fernandes
Joe Fernandes
Albert Gonsalves
J B Gonsalves
John Gonsalves
Bernard Gonsalves
Linus Lopes
Frankie Mathias

Hockey
Francis Xavier Da Costa
Christopher Fernandes
Margaret (Dotsie) Fernandes

Horse-Racing
F I Dias
V C Dias
Carlos Fernandes
Clement Gonsalves
Carl Pereira

Motor Cycle Racing
Desmond D'Andrade

Motor Racing
J Gouveia
Max Jardim
Kit Nascimento
Eric Vieira

Rifle Shooting
Francis F D'Agrella
Lt Col Celso De Freitas
J B Gonsalves

Scouting
F X Da Costa
J A Gomes
J B Gonsalves
Michael Pereira

Table Tennis
Barbara D'Abreu
Desmond De Barros
Vera Lopes

Tennis
Basil Baptista
Doris Baptista
Frank De Caires
Decio De Freitas
Romeo and Muriel Delgado
Margaret Fernandes
Clem Gonsalves
Elvie and Willie Mathias
Louis Mathias
Clarice Menezes
Aggie Mew
Eric Rodrigues

Weightlifting
Bernard Mendonca

Maurice Fernandes. Well known cricketer, 1922.

Suggested Reading re History of Portuguese in Guyana*

Laurence, K O — "The Establishment of the Portuguese Community in British Guiana," *The Jamaican Historical Review*, V, November 1965.

Menezes, Sr M Noel — "Some Preliminary Thoughts on Portuguese Emigration from Madeira to British Guiana," *KYK-Over-A1*, No. 30, December, 1984.

— "The Coming of the Portuguese: From Canefield to Counter," *Sunday Chronicle*, 28 April, 1985, 12 May, 1985 and 19 May, 1985.

Mohamed, Khallel — "Planter Patronage of and Creole Response to the Portuguese Immigrants in British Guiana, 1835-1856," M A Thesis, University of Guyana, 1977.

Moore, Brian L — "The Social Impact of Portuguese Immigration into British Guiana after Emancipation," *A Journal of Latin American and Caribbean Studies*, No. 19, December 1975.

Wagner, Michael J — "Structural Pluralism and the Portuguese in Nineteenth Century British Guiana: A Study in Historical Geography" A Ph.D Thesis McGill University, February 1975.

* To be found at University of Guyana Library.

Little curled feathers on the back of the sky,
– White, chicken-downy on the soft sweet blue, –
In slow reluctant patterns for the world to see.

Then frisky lambs that gambol and bowl along
Shepherded by the brave Trade-wind.

And glittering in the sun come great grave battleships
Ploughing an even keel across the sky.

In their own time, their bowels full of rain
The angry clouds that rage with lightning
Emitting sullen bulldog growls
And then they spirit themselves away in mist and rain.

Over Guiana, Clouds.

And they go rushing on across the country
Staining the land with shadow as they pass,
Closer than raiment to the naked skin, that shadow,
Bringing a pause of sun, over and across
Black noiseless rivers running out to sea,
Fields, pieced and plotted, and ankle deep in rice
Or waving their multitudinous hair of cane.

It scales the sides of mountains
Lifting effortlessly to their summits,
And fleets across savannahs in its race,
But there are times that shadow falters
And hesitates upon a lake
To fix that eye of water in a stare,
Or use its burnished shield to search the sun,
Or yet as maids do,
To let the cloud compose her hurried beauty.
And then upon its way to Venezuela
Across vast stretches where trees huddle close
And throw liana arms around their neighbours.

Over Guiana, Clouds.

Sobre a Guiana, Nuvens.

Poucas plumas encrespadas no dorso do céu.
– Alva penugem sobre o suave e doce azul, –
Lânguido e persistente mostruário para os olhos do mundo.

Alegres cordeiros brincam e saltam ao longo
Pastorados pelos bravos Ventos Alísios.

Tremeluzindo ao sol surgem grandes graves couracados
Lavrando com sua quilha tranqüila através do céu.

A seu próprio tempo, de bojo pojado de chuva
As nuvens raivosas se enfurecem com relâmpagos
Emitindo soturnos rosnados de cão de fila
E desaparecem por magia em bruma e chuva.

Sobre a Guiana, Nuvens.

E vão apressadas através do país
Manchando a terra de sombra ao passar.
Mais justa que as vestes à pele desnuda, sua sombra
Traz uma trégua do sol, aqui e ali
Enegrecve rios silenciosos a correr para o mar,
Campos, unidos e urdidos, e o artelho profundo no arrozal
Ou ondulando a exuberante cabeleira dos canaviais.

Escala as encostas das montanhas
E se ergue sem esforco sobre os cumes,
E passa veloz através das savanas em sua corrida,
Mas há momentos em que a sombra falha
E vacila sobre um lago
Para fixar aquele olho de água espantado,
Ou usa seu escudo polido em busca do sol,
Ou ainda como fazem as donzelas
Deixam a nuvem compor sua efêmera beleza.
No caminho para a Venezuela
Atravessa vastas extensões onde as árvores se enroscam
E se atiram aos braços das lianas ao redor dos vizinhos.

Sobre a Guiana, Nuvens.

[Translated by Zuleika Hallais Walsh – Brazil]

With kind permission
of the author
A J Seymour